BLOOMING UPSIDE DOWN

*A MEMOIR OF HEALING
FROM THE INCURABLE*

LUMALIA ARMSTRONG

CELEBRATE AGAIN BOOKS

Published by Celebrate Again Books, an imprint of Celebrate Again, a platform cultivating transformative remembering through media, events, and holistic and creative services. Founded in 2009. Based in the United States of America. For stocking inquiries, contact hello@celebrateagain.org

This memoir is a personal account of Lumaila Armstrong's life experiences. While names of individuals have been altered for privacy, the events, conversations, and situations portrayed in this book are based on the author's memories and perceptions. Lumalia Armstrong and Celebrate Again cannot guarantee the complete accuracy of every detail, but they have made efforts to ensure the privacy and confidentiality of the individuals involved. Any resemblance to actual persons, living or deceased, or to actual events, locales, or entities is entirely coincidental. Readers are advised that this memoir contains the author's subjective recollections and interpretations. The author and publisher are released from any liability arising from inaccuracies, omissions, or any damages or losses resulting from depicting likelihoods or persons in this memoir. This book is not intended to provide medical advice or treatment. Readers with health concerns are encouraged to seek professional medical guidance and should not use the information provided as a substitute for professional diagnosis or treatment. The author and publisher are in no way liable for any misuse of the material.

Produced by Lumalia Armstrong

celebrateagain.org/books

ISBN: 979-8-9896079-0-7 (paperback) 979-8-9896079-1-4 (ebook)
LCCN: 2023922792

First Edition: January 2024

BLOOMING
UPSIDE
DOWN

CONTENTS

FORWARD

by Dr. Chelsea Page

Years ago, I was expanding my business online and I began seeking photography for new branding photos. I searched many photographers and despite my mind saying otherwise, because of price or something or other, my soul kept guiding me back to Lumalia's website. I'm always looking for ways to deepen my relationship with my soul and the voice of my soul, my intuition, and so I listened. I reached out to schedule an initial phone call, not knowing it would create a profound ripple on both of our lives.

During our first call she asked questions about the photos I desired, my business and who I supported. I remember her softly saying in wonder, "That's me!", as I described her exactly as the ideal woman that I help in coming back home to the truth of their soul. I giggled knowing this is why my soul kept guiding me to her website over all the others. Intuition and divine guidance never ceases to amaze and delight me.

Pictures were later taken by her business partner in Colorado where I live, so I never got the chance to meet Lumalia in person, although our worlds were already weaving together. As time delicately and harshly unfolded over the years for all of us through the Pandemic, I had the honor of guiding Lumalia along her healing journey. I supported her deeply and intimately albeit from a distance in the online world. It's a powerful thing to know lives can be forever changed when you haven't even met in person. Healing knows no time and space. It exists within those that are open to see and be the truth.

As years unfolded, talk of a book emerged and flowed in and out of our conversations. I encouraged her to write in the poetic way her soul desired, and I got to be part of moments like the revelation of the name and the photo that graces the cover with its profound meaning. Until one day, we reached a moment, I'll never forget, when Lumalia asked me to write the forward for her book Blooming Upside Down. I immediately started crying. My whole body and soul lit up and it was one of the easiest yeses I've ever made. Sometimes a moment is all you need for magic.

And now, having witnessed her journey and read the words that dance within the pages of Blooming Upside Down, I'm writing this forward while my head is shaking in awe. In awe of her, her healing from the incurable, and knowing the truth of the energetic footprint this book will leave in the hearts of thousands of others across the world.

If you are looking for a portal into your next level of healing, Blooming Upside Down is it.

Lumalia's memoir is born from deep within her power. The petals of her soul beautifully opened through her healing journey, allowing her to touch upon her naked truth that previously lay hidden for years due to unfathomable trauma and illnesses. Her wisdom is gifted to us within the pages of this book. She is a woman who is so power-ful, even though she is continuously learning to grasp its bigness. It's like a waterfall, which she once said to me, that I myself am the pow-er of a waterfall. But what I know to be true is that power sees power. She is power. She saw it in me and in Blooming Upside Down she helps you see the power in you too, as you splash peacefully in the pools of her wisdom.

If anyone was meant to write a book of profound healing that defies all odds, it's Lumalia. Her expertise that fills the pages comes from her own lived experiences through deep trauma and illnesses that even had doctors scratching their heads. She shares how she tapped into the intelligence held within her own body to allow her-self to fully bloom in a world that was trying to convince her other-wise. Even if that meant doing so upside down.

Lumalia touches deep within her soul, and vulnerably paints her truth of healing on the pages where it feels like she's holding hands with your own soul. Gently and lovingly, she invites you deep into devotion to yourself. Her words are a poetic heaven where the essence of her wisdom plays through the pages like butterflies. Even with the divulging of a life laced in deep and dark traumas, Lumalia artistically weaves her stories amongst the light of love allowing them to easily slide down softly into your soul.

Unlike traditional "how to's" and memoirs on healing, Lumalia brings to you the lessons and discovery of truths she's learned on her healing journey in a delicate yet profound offering. The lessons are artfully woven in her stories where they are all gathered into a beauti-ful bouquet, guiding you along with a gentle invitation for stun-ning contemplations on how these lessons can be applied to your own healing.

The unique format of Blooming Upside Down also allows each chapter to be a stand-alone, which adds to the enriching power of the book. It provides an opportunity for you to play with your intuition and open to any page your soul is guiding you to receive the wisdom within. This beautifully mirrors the healing journey; one that is not linear and predictable. Instead, it's rather unexpected and delightfully non-traditional: The Booming Upside Down way of healing.

I truly believe our world is needing a new perspective on healing. On growing. On accessing deep within what is our naked truth in a world that conditions us into a lie. Blooming Upside Down is that new perspective.

I trust and know that, just as Lumalia and I landed in each other's worlds in an unpredictable destiny moment that has changed both of our lives forever, this book finding you will do the same. And so, with not much more delay, I delightfully invite you to gently walk into and explore the pages inside Blooming Upside Down.

Let the words kiss your soul as it did mine.

Let the tears flow like waterfalls down your cheeks like it did mine.

Let the loving embrace of her profound poetic words tickle your skin and absorb delicately into your body and soul as it did mine.

Let yourself Bloom Upside Down.

- Dr. Chelsea Page
Intimacy expert and psychologist
drchelseapage.com

INTRODUCTION

Paused. Stillness within a
moment demands you must *inhale*
and breathe in every single sense
surrounding you. Some call that magical
moment a space where love blossoms. Still, the
same is true when discovering the truth of something
your soul has known deeply but never noticed until it meets
the equal of its kind, matching the mysterious energies deep within
us as humans.

I stood before her in the curated greenhouse at an old mansion
now turned tourist museum. She called me from across the country,
then across the walkway, to stare her eye to eye and call her beloved:

The Medinilla Magnifica.

It was in year three of the seven that I was really sick that my mother invited me and my daughter, Olea, along with my sister Sara, to a girl's trip to Asheville, North Carolina, to tour the Biltmore mansion and enjoy the great smoky mountains. It had been years since I traveled. But I adored traveling, and my mom offered to cover our costs.

During the trip to Asheville, we arranged to have a wheelchair when needed. We planned a schedule that included afternoon naps for Olea and me and the ability to make our own food. My doctors had given me the green light for the journey, but every step was an effort.

We flew into Atlanta and drove up through South Carolina. Stopping at a waterfall, I felt my heart come alive for the first time in years after being mostly stuck at home. Witnessing so much rushing beauty spraying against every one of my limbs helped my body remember it was still alive. After stopping there, we went through the winding roads into the Smoky Mountains.

My mom rented us a little blue cottage with white shingles and grass all around. It was a cozy space with a patio, a neighborhood cat Olea fell in love with, and a small bedroom where she and I would share. By late morning, we ventured out to the Biltmore mansion, exploring the house as we listened to the pre-recorded audio for each room.

Olea, only four, ran up and down every corridor, spinning in her turquoise dress and black ballet shoes my mom bought, fueling her love for new shoes and twirling skirts. My mom happily chased after her throughout the house while Sara and I paused to listen to the history of this old American home.

After we went through the house, we went to the gardens, finding a lush medley of colors and fragrances, sending your eyes into a firework of color explosions. It was October, but everything was still green and slowly entering fall as leaves began to crunch under our feet along with the pebbled, graveled paths. We paused in a deep section of grass to take a photo together under a large willow tree with the Biltmore mansion framed in the background.

All of us had dressed up to tour this fancy house. Olea wore her dress. I had a green skirt and compression tights to help my limbs and blood pressure stay inside my heart. Sara wore nice black slacks and a silk blouse, her thick, straight blonde hair on her shoulders. My mom had a sparkling sweater, her blonde hair mixed with silver streaks tied into a braid framing her face. It was the perfect moment for a gathering of three generations of women, melting my mom's heart with her ear-to-ear smile. She is someone who has always adored family. Meanwhile, I was sparked with the joy of exploration.

As we made our way through the gardens, I paused to take pictures of all the beautiful greenery, the arches covered in vines, the manufactured bushes shaped perfectly into statues and hedges, the roses still blooming, fragrant with their signature scent radiating through the air. Then, the rain threatened to send us inside as the dew clung to the air with its beautiful, sweet smell. Soon, the rain began to pour down, so we quickly moved inside the greenhouse, kept up by local gardeners in the spirit of the original Vanderbilt owners.

We began meandering through the greenhouse, my mom asking Olea to pause in front of so many flowers for pictures as she happily ate up all the attention like she was being given chocolate cake. I noticed some beautiful orchids, making Olea pause for a photo in an archway with palm trees rising to the tall greenhouse ceilings.

As she ran off to catch my mom, I turned to my left, and something caught my eye. It was unlike anything I had ever seen before. This magenta flower with strings and bulbs at the end of her bloom grew not up but down.

Never had I seen such beauty. This flower's vivid pink radiated against the dark contrast of the greenery softly framing her. It was as if darkness had to exist around her just so you'd notice the rare neo-pink color she created to stand out among the rest of the lavish creatures growing inside this greenhouse. Astounded and befuddled that such a beautiful thing could exist, I pulled out my camera to photograph this flower, declaring her something I wanted to keep. Some promise within me saw that she held a part of me, but it wouldn't be until years later that I would understand why she caught my eye.

As soon as we got home, I edited the hundreds of photos I'd taken. Once I returned to the photograph of the pink-neo flower, I saved her as the background on my phone. Something in me wanted to keep her in my pocket. I didn't think much of it at the time; she just seemed beautiful.

For so long, I tried to figure out what flower she was, but no one knew.

It wasn't until significant time had passed that I realized what drew me to this stunning flower. It was how her resilience reflected back my own story of growing in the middle of so much darkness, being so sick with so little hope of getting better. She held this profound metaphor that despite growing, in what I deemed an unconventional way (upside down), she was still the most beautiful flower I'd ever witnessed. Despite being surrounded by a mother who adores flowers and cultivated a yard full of them in the desert sandy soil, I had never beheld such breathtaking glory in all my years.

Not only did this flower's beauty shine but her ability to bloom upside down was reflected back to me in one of the darkest times of my own life. Maybe I, too, could become that marvelous, even if it felt like I no longer knew which way gravity was supposed to hold me. She became my hope, unknowingly, as she lived in the background on my phone for the next five years, while I wrestled with finding my feet again after literally being thrown to the ground with chronic illnesses, generational trauma, and the overwhelm of motherhood in our modern day. Each time I saw her beauty, I was given a spark of hope that things could get better.

Sitting in my therapist's office while I was sick, she asked me, "What helps you process your experiences?"

I replied confidently, "Writing. I've always loved writing."

"You should share more about your experiences. There are places you can share online."

She then gave me a list of places where I could share, which I did. Until one day, I began writing more in-depth about everything I'd been through.

Sharing my stories opened spaces in me I didn't know were there. By sharing my journey, I knew I could heal, and so could others.

Despite what the doctors said, I knew I'd figure out how to be whole again.

A few years later, I came back to writing after a business coach recommended I write down what my future would look like. As I began to heal a little bit, I dove deep into my first love of photography, trying my best to find a way to stay in business despite my disabilities. My ability to share my stories is what kept my business afloat. As I began to navigate what was next for my career as I shifted out of photography into wanting to teach more, I fell in love with telling my story again.

After being mostly healed from all my debilitating symptoms, I decided to write this book. I knew that in a world full of so much gloom, others needed to know that they, too, could bloom amidst darkness and defy the norms.

During the season of beginning to write this book, I had this flower return to me, knowing deep within she had to be the cover. Something about the way she grew gave me hope to get through what I'd experienced. Though I couldn't always put my finger on what it was about her, it felt as if she was a silent angel watching over me, cheering me on to keep growing—even if it felt hard and horrific.

Shortly after, I shared this photograph of her during a chat with a mastermind group, saying, "I want this flower to be my book cover."

At that exact moment, Lisbet, a woman on the call from Switzerland, declared, "Wait, hold on." She removed herself from the screen as we all heard footsteps and clattering in the background. She returned with the same flower I had photographed four years before. "You mean the Medinilla Magnifica?"

My whole body felt goosebumps up to my eyelids. Everyone on the call shouted, "Oh my god. Are you serious?!" Thrill shot through my body as tears filled my eyes.

Of course, she was called Magnifica because that is what my journey has been: absolutely magnificent.

Deep within my soul, I knew after meeting this flower that if she could bloom upside down—*so could I.*

In the beautiful journey of putting this manuscript together, I, in full tears of stunning joy, realized this book could mirror the Healing Roadmaps tool inside Celebrate Again, my company that originally started as a photography business but has now morphed into a platform for transformative remembering through media, events, holistic, and creative services. The Healing Roadmaps pulls together all the healing modalities I adore into one experience—a guide I wish I would have had in my own journey. So I made it for us, for you.

You'll notice this book follows a similar theme. And with it, I encourage you to witness the highs and lows I take you on by sharing my non-conventional story, one without a structured story arch, but one that my heart calls us to receive deep into the belly of listening, and births us out into remembering the majesty in each of us.

The journey is yours to take. You can read it straight through, flip to any chapter you want to soak in the story you need for that day, or trust your pull to whatever titles and sections you are called into. There is no wrong journey. Trust your curiosities. After all, your intention is your greatest gift.

I am celebrating *your* unique journey, as well as *mine.*

SPARK

AWARENESS IS THE
BEGINNING OF A
MAGICAL
LIFE

YOUR BODY IS FULL OF INFINITE WISDOM

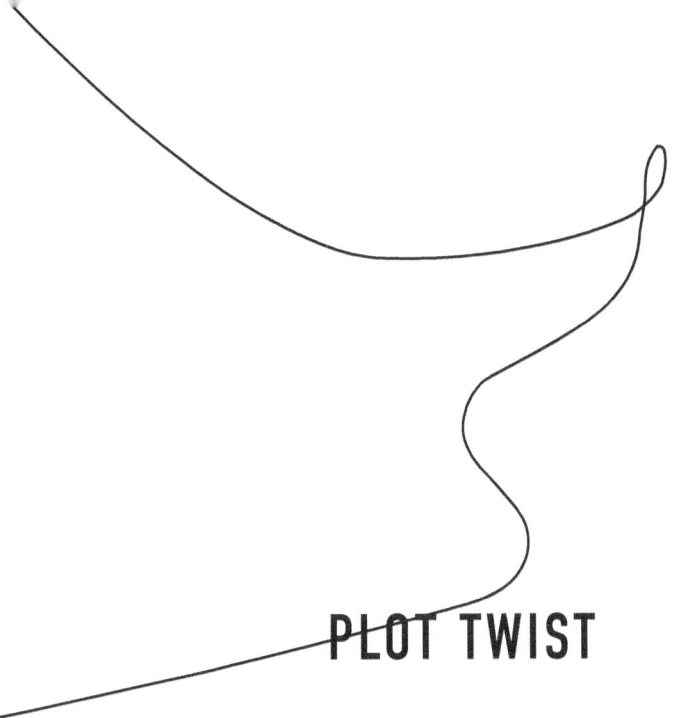

PLOT TWIST

As I try to sit and recount my life, I'm faced with the challenge that no matter how much we've been through, how we define ourselves is never entirely clear. Our cells are constantly duplicating, expanding, and writing new stories daily. How can we fully define ourselves since we are daily beholding?

Beholding. It's such a powerful word. It means to pause with observation and notice something especially remarkable. What a wonderful world we'd live in if we all learned to *behold ourselves.*

On the surface, I had a magical childhood. I loved fashion; I'd draw dresses that would make any girl swoon. There were dance moves that saturated my bedroom floor as I made up dances to NSYNC, swearing I would be a famous choreographer one day. And while that didn't come true, I had the honor of choreographing a few original pieces for student theater productions. Creativity ruled my world, from my exploits as an architect using legos, to creating unique furniture and houses, instead of the step-by-step rocket ship instructions provided. All of these childhood dreams and experiences became my reality later in life, turning a small photography business into a thriving culture-shifting experience brand catapulting individuals to bliss and harmony, allowing them to step into their prerogative of creativity.

However, beneath the surface, the actual events of my childhood depicted a dark picture. One I didn't know was painted and buried deep inside my body until my late twenties and early thirties.

Throughout childhood, I ran barefoot through the streets, my imagination leading the way, joy filling my lungs, dancing, laughing, and always smiling. Cookie Monster sneaker extraordinaire, little did I know my love for desserts and the freedom to devour them with vigor protected my brain, holding on to so much for me.

A therapist once shared that considering all I had been through, it was remarkable that my personality hadn't fractured into two separate identities to cope; confirming that I did not have Dissociative Identity Disorder. Most people who've experienced the level of trauma I went through as a child, which I didn't discover until my late twenties, statistically, are the ones who develop a Dissociative Disorder to cope with their realities. Part of the mind is present during the abuse, to manage other self-like part(s) created to exist outside of the trauma. Somehow, this wasn't me, but by all means of stats, it should have been.

However, I've found that I have this magical gift of taking anything horrific and turning it into pure gold, while holding every ounce of debris with tenderness, affirmation, and empathy; seeing its use and role in my story without judgment and with observation.

Looking back, I saw how I'd taken my father's verbal abuse and how it's helped me realize I have zero tolerance for abusive talk. The more I understood the abuse I went through, the more I began to understand the way I spoke negatively to my daughter, my husband, and myself was not okay. I turned the words of any criticism into a checkpoint for myself instead of purging it onto the nearest other.

This childhood abuse became the magnifying glass through which I could filter out all the lies. These lies naturally overflowed onto others, but I eventually changed them into truths by noticing them first in myself before they hurt anyone around me. I could turn the abuse into the tool by which I examined myself, opening me up to more profound love and affection.

Instead of splitting into fragmented parts, my early work was focused on untangling all of the complex threads of existence. I saw my younger self, the one locked away in a part of my brain, and the details of my body that grew to ache, swell, fester, and literally boil, all labeled later as chronic illnesses.

Sexually abused by my father, I found out later in my life he was also from a similar lineage of abusers. Generation after generation, parents stealing away from their children what was never theirs. It's repeated itself over and over again. And if we know one thing as humans, history repeats itself. Until someone chooses a new way to be. Deep in my soul, I knew I had to become the plot twist, altering the trajectory of generations-old narrative. History would never believe it, but I was at the end of this storyline. Being the plot twist became my self-proclaimed birthright, and I owned it with every fiber of my being. I would be the end of all the abuse.

With this vigor deep in my subconscious, I tried everything differently, and when told to give up, I tried again and again.

Even though I was culturally ingrained by the Christian church to stay married no matter the cost due to vows I "made before God," I chose my right to be happy. I wanted my daughter to witness what healthy love looked like. When doctors told me they had no cure for the illnesses that debilitated my life, I sought every alternative option until I found the one that brought back more of my life. This is me, having practiced the plot twists over and over again.

Throughout my childhood, I listened to my cravings for staying connected to the earth despite my grandmother's pleas to wear shoes and wash my feet more, while also fueling my brain with sugar to remain whole. As I began to learn how to listen to my body in my late twenties, I thought I never knew how to listen, to really listen, to my body. But now I see that I've always paid attention—by fueling it with what I learned: sugar to keep me whole. Knowing what I know now about the body, this extreme sugar addiction kept my brain from developing Dissociative Identity Disorder. I had enough fuel for it to keep going. As I entered an emotionally abusive marriage, my body's voice grew louder and louder, buried under obligation and "shoulds" to the vows I made under Christianity, along with the fear of not wanting to ruin my daughter. But I called bull shit eventually and said no fucking more. So now, in the listening of my deep soul, I've found my sovereignty.

Frequently, when I look back on my body's journey through life, I'm proud of all the roads I've traveled. All the wear and tear, all this life that has held me so sacredly to. I love how it holds every memory; its holy role in my journey inside this Milky Way glow we call living. Despite all I've been through, I hear my soul shouting, "Darling, we are made for freedom, and we've already got every ounce of it in this earth-worn vessel. It's right here inside of us, waiting to shine."

There was a time when I would have said my childhood was somber, and parts of it were very dark. Being sexually abused by my father and male relatives, addicted to pornography in elementary school; while raised to be codependent, verbally abused, and manipulated, was anything but light. These memories were so dark. It wasn't until I stepped into more light and safety that they even unfolded into my consciousness. It was a dark season, the birthing of a seed planted deep where no one saw the growth and the agony of the shell breaking open. It's a lonely and brutal process—the hardest growth one must endure.

But look at me now, this tree growing its ancient roots, a lighthouse shining for all to marvel and adore, but never fueled by their adoration, planted by streams and sustaining our own light.

Untangling the complex threads of abuse over the years, today, I stand reborn and transformed. I learned how to listen and communicate my own needs. I discovered boundaries internally and externally. I linked my illnesses to beliefs and imprisoned trauma cells, slowly recovering them with love and safety. I began to build a life of security, calm, and trust. And am less haunted by the sexual abuse, fully able to enjoy intimacy on my body's terms.

I found the greatest love of my life, who does not have the abusive highs and lows, wondering if my husband will love me today or tomorrow because I now feel and hear it daily. My daughter gets to witness what safe, secure, and beautiful love really is. My body is less reactive to illnesses, maintaining more of its boundaries. I am showing up every single day to remember I am the generational plot twist.

SWOLLEN

If only I could feel the surge of life coursing through my veins. Yet, I find myself burdened by a body swollen with avoidance, suppressing the story I've longed to shout, "Look at me," projecting an image of wild freedom as I traverse the world on four wheels, dance under the sun's warm embrace, and dip my toes into every ocean, except the distant expanse of the Indian, which feels just out of reach.

Yet, deep within, a little girl cowers in the corner, yearning for the solace of comforting arms and whispered reassurances. I turned to my father, the one who had made her feel utterly alone in search of validation. But his response echoed dismissive demands for greater effort, as if my growth could only be achieved through his manipulative provisions. "Give me what I want, and I'll give you what you need."

Seeking love elsewhere, I poured out my affection, hoping my first husband, Micah, would reciprocate it. Instead, it was a well that ran dry, leaving me withered on the floor until I found the strength to rise, seeking solace in the crisp mountain air, as the gusts of wind urged me to confront the fragments of myself still trapped in that bed of despair.

Crawling and groping my way forward, I finally mustered the courage to ask for help, never ceasing in my search. The day arrived when the right voices began to sing, reminding me not to surrender; assuring me that this was not the only story I had to live. It was a moment of choice—picking one from a kaleidoscope of possibilities.

Now, I stand here, brimming with life that has left me breathless. I reach inward and gently ask the little girl stuck in the corner of my heart, "What do you need?"

Uncertainty clouds my mind. "Am I enough? Am I worthy of holding her? Can I provide the support she yearns for when I barely stand alone?" But with tenderness, I lean in and press a kiss upon her cheek, feeling the wetness of oceans she has traversed in her attempts to drown, only to discover her own buoyancy.

This is not the end of our story.

Together, hand in hand, we embark on a journey, seeking refuge in a hammock beneath the shade of a tree. We snuggle together, dreaming of the countless sunsets we will paint with our words as the sand beneath our feet fills with others, drawn by the enchanting tales we have to share—stories we know, made just for her and I, just for us to tell.

RESCUING THE LISTENER'S VOICE

Sometimes, we're absolutely terrible listeners to our bodies, our inner wisdom, and our life experiences. And we're taught this. Our minds are labeled as our most precious gift, praised as the gateway to freedom. Yet, culturally, we are hardly ever trained to listen to ourselves, let alone our bodies, heaven forbid.

Even after a decade of battling illnesses, a profound part of me has never really believed, "This is my life now." I've never accepted this life with autoimmune diseases entirely as my new way of existence. It proclaims that I will forever be more sensitive than others to everything. I must be hypervigilant because my immune system isn't as strong as others. And I'm so thankful a piece of me has never accepted this as truth despite my wrestling with it.

I once read in a book by a Western psychologist, those who have experienced childhood sexual abuse often struggle with boundaries to the point that even the immune system "may fail to appropriately recognize invading organisms."[1] I believed this to be my truth of all the truths. Part of my story has been lacking discernment and seeing the truth. In some ways, I've lived behind a veil between the life I lived and the life that happened to my body, the one forgotten by my mind to protect me to keep going until it saw it was safe enough to show me again.

Yet it was there in the hidden pieces, that I hid a significant part of myself.

I remember being seated at the dinner table with my parents when I was seven. Craving more of their attention, I tried to tell them the exciting parts of my day. But they were so engrossed in talking about their workdays to each other that they wouldn't listen. This had become so familiar. I promised myself at that moment to stop trying to tell them anything. They wouldn't listen, so I just stopped talking to them.

I've never been particularly close with either of my parents, and now I know more deeply why. It wasn't that they didn't listen. It wasn't that I stopped using my voice. It wasn't that I was neglected. It was that I was told to keep quiet. Not just at the dinner table, or when I wanted to scream when I was angry, or when I blurted out my song during a family vacation open mic night that apparently shattered glasses. It was every time a family member stole my body, I was told to keep quiet.

So I did. I lost my voice. I became quiet. I became the calm one. Just observing, noticing. In my twenties, when I became a photographer, I became the seer but not the speaker. I buried my truths deep inside because it was the only way I knew how to survive. Little did I know at the time, in it, I buried my deepest treasure, my Voice, my power.

Photography provided a sacred space. I captured the love I craved, unable to create it within my first marriage. I desired a love that was powerful and fierce. Witnessing it felt safe, even if only in my mind. My mind was my sanctuary, my body, a tool.

When I was younger, my cousin was very sick. She was always in and out of hospitals with treatments, and near-death experiences. My family gave her full attention and rallied around her.

I saw it then. This is how you become powerful, noticed, and given attention. So, I let my discerning stop. I allowed my body to become like my cousin's, who had all the attention slowly and with time.

Looking back, I was okay with never having my family's attention. I found it in friends, other parents, teachers, and communities. I found people to listen and see me.

But then, I entered a marriage with a profoundly hurting boy named Micah at the age of twenty and twenty one. Micah could never see much of me, nor was I capable of letting myself even be fully seen. However, I deeply saw Micah. I fell in love with how he would let me rescue him from his suffering. I saw my Voice come to life. Yet I made it worth being his power instead of my own.

Micah often said in the hundreds of letters we wrote each other, "Thank you for always talking me off the cliff." Many psychologists call this trauma bonding, replicating our childhood wounds to try and resolve them with someone else. Instead, we typically clone them, inevitably retraumatizing ourselves. And this is precisely what I did. Micah heard my Voice, my power, but he did not see me.

In a way, he became my parents, ignoring me as if I was unable to be fully seen. So, I went back to this discovery I found. If only I were so sick, he would have to love me, and stay with me. This wasn't done consciously but as a breaking of any other truth I ever knew. I wanted to be loved so desperately by this man that I used the one thing I learned early on: to make everyone else put aside their own struggles to love and express care to someone else who is needing the other's attention as they hopelessly suffer.

After Micah pursued an affair, the illnesses started. My nervous system began to break down, unable to hold everything I'd experienced. I first began to get dizzy spells amidst the heartbreak I was experiencing. For the next three years, my body began to speak louder and louder. After the traumatic birth of our daughter Olea, followed by the most challenging first year of her sleepless life, my digestion issues amplified; hardly any food seemed to sit well with me. On top of that, I broke out in incurable rashes. My joints began to ache, causing pain and swelling that radiated from the daily use of my hands. I frequently felt fatigued, having difficulty walking more than a quarter-mile at a time.

Until Olea was two, I often passed out on our kitchen floor. Low blood pressure and high heart rates left me unpredictably disabled for the next four years. My limbs would often go numb when I slept, causing me to lose use of them for periods of time. I slept in compression wear to try to keep the blood flowing.

The months and years that followed led to full-body rashes that felt like a living hell fire. I was wheelchair bound for a month and primarily bedridden without mobility in my wrist. I was incapable of walking far distances for years, and unable to mother normally. As I reached for care, I kept being told my immune system wasn't working normally. I was cautioned by physicians that I had to be extra careful not to get more infections, which I often did. Coughs lingering longer than they should, female infections lasted months, and all of them were non-responsive to traditional forms of treatment.

After a year of what felt like hundreds of experts offices, I finally received a diagnosis: Palindromic Rheumatism, an autoimmune disease that is often a precursor to Rheumatoid Arthritis and Dysautonomia or P.O.T.S, standing for Postural Orthostatic Tachycardia Syndrome. The doctors wanted to continue to name all the symptoms not within the scope of either of these, but I was tired of spending my life in their offices. As I learned, Dysautonomia is a literal breakdown of the nervous system, the web of connection between our heart and mind. I realized later that the severing happened in my grief, cutting off my truths from my body.

Yet, in my soul's wisdom, it used this. It became the pausing required of me that brought me back to my depths and truths. I needed so much care that I could no longer exist in American culture's chaos; I had to go in and listen—listen to my Voice. I had to love me, and learn to care deeply. I had to give myself the attention I always craved, the listening I always longed for.

It's taken almost a decade on the most beautiful journey to return to me. To become the parent across the table who listens intently to the stories of my soul, to give myself a Voice. To grieve deeply over the horrific harm done to me, to anger, to rid myself of toxic patterns and environments, and to trust and receive the relationship I knew existed. And to boldly reclaim the power I so cleverly hid behind in the veil of suffering, I thought I needed to receive deep love.

I wonder how many of us believe in so much unneeded suffering, owning a truth that we must sacrifice to be loved.

But what if we loved ourselves so deeply that we attract the most amazing people, as we create a web of unconditional love that is not dependent on our neediness, and instead grows purely because we exist?

Ancient texts advocate this. It's time to recycle them and remember the sacred truths within our souls—suffering does not deepen belonging. Our unique attention and expression of Voice attracts and gives all the love we could ever desire.

---

1. Anodea Judith, "Eastern Body Western Mind," 134.

FRANKENSTEIN AT FIRST

Maybe you keep writing beautiful metaphors
because it feels like Frankenstein;
unsafe for you to share your truth.

Not because you aren't brave enough,
or because you are still bleeding out on the hospital bed
after your car accident called childhood sexual abuse
from more men in your family than your memory will uncover
for your own sanity,
who their fathers also abused;
uncles, pastors, and maybe the leader of the cult
your grandmother, Betty, was also a part of but left
because she couldn't sacrifice her son.

                              Thank god she said *no* for once.
No, maybe you keep hiding behind metaphors because
you were told by your mother Germaine that you must be sorry

for the way you make everyone feel by refusing to give a fuck
when your sister Sara tells you you are an anorexic tomboy,
hoping subconsciously that if you stopped being so pretty,
they will all stop touching you.

You stop dancing in the kitchen for your grandmother Julia,
and start wearing band t-shirts to concerts,
hoping to become one of the nice and sad skater boys.

No, maybe you keep hiding behind the beautiful figure of speech
because you're afraid the world isn't ready to handle your verity.

And they aren't.

But your body cannot hold it anymore.
It's purging too much of its nutrients.
The banana cleanses, and the juicing isn't working.
But the doctors keep saying nothing is wrong
as you whisper to yourself,
it's because I keep hiding
it
all.

So today, you say **no more**, and you begin to spill it *all*/like vomit.

Until every last ounce of you can
stand upright again and finally begin to tell the truth,
no matter how Frankenstein it may feel at first.

UNLEARNING HOW TO GHOST MYSELF

I positioned myself by the window. I had walked over there as my favorite tunes blared, searching for music to help me process through movement. The clouds hung low like the dream catcher over my bedroom door. I hear they hold lots of water so they look so fluffy, like sky marshmallows. I bet they are blueberry-flavored. I began to move with that same flavor lingering on my tongue from a smoothie I had just swallowed.

For the past sixteen hours, I had been submerged in a pit of emotions, not sure when or if I would resurface. The urge to let myself sink deeper into my pillow, to drown in the cushion's softness, was potent.

Despite this, I persisted in listening to my inner self. I allowed the pent-up feelings to find their voice, having just shown someone new in my life my actual state, right here in the depths where vulnerability was a rare sight.

I poured my heart onto these pages, as my emotions spilled freely. I asked myself, "What do you need, my dear?"

As I stepped toward the window, a screen separated me from the outside world. I noticed the sun's attempt to slice through the clouds; closing my eyes, I pretended she would.

A brief sliver of sunlight warmed my skin. In the window's reflection, I caught sight of armor glistening all over my skin. I told her to wear the warrior's clothes because it would make me strong.

I had always considered myself the strongest; viewing emotions and tears as signs of weakness. My mother was emotionless my whole life, it seemed. She only cried once in my entire childhood when my cousin Heather died after battling cancer for twenty years of her short life.

This old mindset had fostered connections with men more quickly than with women. I often found my internal dialogue saying, "Push harder. Use brute force. Everything is solvable if you try hard enough and you just keep going."

But this was just the clothing I was told to wear. It wasn't just an extra jacket to protect me from the cold. It was a refined metal, molded to my contours, designed to protect me.

I tried to put it on for my Moon, my new boyfriend. He sweetly saw it and said, "Nope, I don't need that from you."

I protested with a defiant glare, "Why won't you let me be fake strong?" It was then that I felt the burden this armor imposed.

But I understand it now—I don't require this armor any longer.

For too long, I had been Superman, outfitted in my shiny suit, rescuing those who allowed themselves to be saved. But it had come at a cost, exhausting every ounce of my being. I'm still rummaging through the trash where I tossed it all to find the lost parts.

My Moon desired Clark Kent, while I defaulted to being Superman. But did I really want to put that cape back on?

I did not.

The cape had grown heavy. I longed for a royal gown, dancing under the stars, feeling the sand between my toes, and inhaling the earthy scent of moss drenched in the rain.

I desired to gaze at the clouds, share laughs over silly jokes, and float in the ocean's embrace. This time, I was hand in hand with my Moon and hand in hand with myself. Every moment I am cherished as if it were the most extraordinary day, enveloped in wonder and awe.

Ready to undress, I gazed at my reflection as it illuminated the window. The light bounced off me. Revealing, not the darkness that seeks light, but the interplay between my hands and shirt; an acknowledgment of how I faded behind armor, just as light does behind the clouds. No longer do I require that light to be seen. I don't need to struggle like a wrestler facing tigers to prove my worth. I will no longer keep ghosting myself. I will keep dancing so my light continues illuminating me, reminding me I'm the one who gets to remember my inherent wholeness.

BRAVERY MADE ME NUMB

I'll stand here with my cape blowing in the w $_i$ n ^{d} .
I've always had the courage to take the first le a   p.

I've always been the one
the first to jump off that clif$_f$,

but I don't want to anymore.
I don't want to be adored
for the marvelous I do.

I want to hold *your* hand
and ju^{m}p with you.
To gaze at each other
right before we take that st^{e}p
and catch each other
when the air pocketed b^{u}b$_b$le$_s$
cradle us to the surface.
And we'll share the same air
of feeling alive together.

I AM THE DARKNESS

The world suddenly plunged into darkness, despite the radiant sun, as clear skies graced the heavens seconds prior. There I was, reclining on my trusty picnic blanket, a permanent resident of my whimsically labeled "adventure trunk." I've always believed that real adventure embraces messiness—a touch of the weird and a willingness to break the etiquette rules of what you've been told you "should" do.

At my cherished local park, Mt. Tabor, I lay on my back near the overlook of a reservoir that peaked into the whole city of Portland. The evergreen trees seemingly hugged my back, just a few feet of surround-sound behind me. The birds sang their song off in the distance as I was cozy on my gray blanket. My shirt was playfully tucked under my bra, revealing the gleaming expanse of my pale belly. It had been months since my skin had been kissed by the golden rays. My sky-stretched arms moved in a dance, drawing me into meditation. My eyes closed suddenly, and the sunlight disappeared.

In an instant, the world turned from day to night. I opened my eyes only to find reality unaltered, couples strolling ahead on the trail with not a cloud in sight, bees sucking the nectar of the cherry blossoms, and moms with children sticking their noses in the same delight. However, one thing was different. My arm had unconsciously positioned itself to block my eyes from the sun, an inadvertent metaphor for my ongoing struggle.

Believing in my own sufficiency has always been a battle. I've collected achievements as if they were badges: a GPA beyond 4.0 with honors, the hard-won successes of opening businesses across multiple states, overcoming debilitating symptoms of chronic illness, liberating myself from a toxic relationship, and embracing the role of a single mother; all while birthing new entrepreneurial ventures, and merging lives with the love of my life.

Yet, deep inside me, I ask, "Is this enough?"

It's as if each achievement is a mere stepping stone toward a mythical destination where the masculine wound will finally be soothed, honey-coated, and whispered to, "My dear, you can go rest now."

However, life imposed its own version of rest. During the years I grappled with illness, I confronted every inner demon in the closet of my heart: moths, dragons, and tiny warrior creatures shooting arrows down from the top, declaring, "You shall not enter."

I wrestled too much,
as I mostly found a gentleness within that opened the gate,
an entry ticket that allowed the bridge to drop,
and an invitation to enter.

Despite my growth, surrender, and self-permission to be whole, I still find myself in the loop of pushing, striving, and hoping for movement. It's as if my arm, instead of any external forces, casts a shadow over the light. It is a frustrating cycle, like a broken record that is stuck repeating the same tune over and over.

I know it's not the complete truth. I have transformed, embracing the gentleness that acknowledges my worthiness and my enoughness, every day.

At my park, I inquired within, asking, "What do you need?"

I unearthed a revelation: whenever I'm granted the freedom to pursue anything, I tend to overcommit, losing the essence of my being. I sacrifice everything for something outside of myself, a pattern that can no longer continue.

As my arm blocked the sun, I learned this is a lesson on healing, an unraveling of the tale that began in the shadows of an abused childhood. We were taught through our stolen bodies that giving of ourselves to the other is how we know love. So, we crave the validation of others to know our worth. It's a tragedy concealed beneath the menagerie of human existence, one that cries out for closure.

The curtain must fall on this repetitive act. This cannot go on or repeat. It has been going on far too long. So I'm learning with each day to choose gentleness for myself. I am learning that healing is truly more about learning to look inside, than out.

NO EXIT PLAN

As I settled into her office, a little cubby of a room tucked inside a church building, I sank into a squishy couch adorned with comforting pillows and tissues within an easy reach. She sat across from me, as she rubbed her sore hands that knew the same pain as mine—ache before old age. Katie Jo was one of the many influential therapists I worked with over the years. Still, more than that, she knew what it meant for a body to hurt before its natural decaying time.

Katie Jo had her dark hair tucked back into a ponytail and a blanket tossed over her lap. She asked me that day, as I sat on her couch, "What if you felt what you're feeling?" Her gaze held mine; inviting, raw, honest.

My response burst out as if it would somehow escape my ability to do what she asked me. "I'm afraid I'm going to drown."

Her simple acknowledgment, "A lot of people fear that too," lingered in the air; leaving me to wonder if this fear is why we seek refuge in numbness.

We're afraid of the pain. Afraid of the emotions that seem like they will drown us because they are so big. They feel overwhelming and out of control. So we push them down further, flooding them with to-do's, entertainment, or food; anything that will stuff us full, wishing it was all a cotton ball, soaking up the igniting fuel of the flame that just needs to burn.

Sadly, no cotton ball exists.

Eventually, the food will stop working, the entertainment will grow weary, or we'll become tired of feeling numb. These are the coping mechanisms we've used to keep living. But the funny thing about coping mechanisms is they are safety pins holding up pants that don't fit. We need a sewing machine carefully crafted to size everything together. We need more tools because those coping strategies certainly don't mend.

Maybe it's not a sewing machine we need, but the gentleness of the hand that comes to thread it all together.

Once I poured my heart out as I shared my story and my journey with others, I wished they would look me in the eye and weep with me. I didn't know then that's what I needed. I mostly received blank faces like a deer about to meet its fate in a car's headlights on the back country roads at night. I knocked the air out of everyone. My story left everyone speechless.

I remember sitting in Tiffany's living room with another woman from my church small group while our kids played on the floor as a few more were happily napping in their rooms. Tiffany and her husband loved renovating, so their home was constantly in transition as they redesigned their kitchen, fireplace, and floor. This week, it was the kitchen that needed cupboard covers. Despite having three kids under four, she was always so put together, and her house floor was visible. She was also an exhausted mother, asked to do too much in the name of being a good Christian wife, raising babies alone in ways we used to raise them in tribes. In our little church community, we did our best to be each other's tribe. Still, we were all in the same season: little kids, married for a handful of years, late twenties to thirties, trying to make sense of the world.

We sat on her couch, ignoring the kid's needs just for a few moments to talk. She looked into my eyes and asked kindly, "How are you doing?"

Mothers know this rarity of silence. It's as if we can be honest instead of giving our standard American reply. "I'm good," plastered with a smile we've all practiced, like the waiters who are exhausted from serving everyone with false emotions. So I told her the truth.

"Micah has been drinking again. I don't feel safe with him anymore. The other day, Olea almost got hurt because he wasn't paying attention. I don't trust him with her when I have to be gone on the weekends photographing weddings."

She stared me in the eyes, doe-eyed and apologetic. "That sounds hard. I'm sorry. Chris sometimes drinks too, but mostly I overdo it."

We quickly moved on as if I hadn't just bombed her with my deepest fear.

This happened repeatedly with everyone. I told the truth about what was happening in my life and felt helpless about what to do.

Others had advice to give, too, because their response wasn't to freeze but to fight. They'd come at me intensely with everything I could do to force the pain that made them so uncomfortable away as soon as possible. But it never did. It never would.

Our responses to pain and hardship are primal. They are human and expected.

Years later, I got off a phone call with a couple wanting me to be their photographer. They told me some of their stories, "We're getting married because Joe almost died. He got COVID really badly. I couldn't see him in the hospital, and we thought we would lose each other. So we decided to skip all the normal wedding plans to celebrate being together."

I wanted to weep with them but knew I had to stay on the topic of being their elopement photographer. I couldn't imagine the struggle of what they went through. I was so tempted to numb, block off, and hold steady. But as soon as I hung up the phone call, I wept. I grieved for all of us who have endured the horrific and the unimaginable. I wished I experienced this with others as I shared my story in the thick of it.

I want to say that when they shared the hardship and horror, we all embraced each other and wept—declaring with our unspoken wails this wasn't okay. Expressing with our whole bodies that this isn't right, that we're sorry. I wish we wouldn't apologize with our words but our tears instead.

I no longer need that because I let myself rain. I've held my story, known of its hardship, and see this wasn't okay. I walked hand in hand, telling every part of me that couldn't be supported by my family, community, or friends, "It's not okay. But I'm here now, ready to hold and heal whatever we can."

I wonder what would have happened if every friend I shared my story with, when I couldn't hold a mug or button my pants, or sleep at night because rashes covered my skin in searing pain that threatened to take my life, held my hand and wept with me. Would I have felt less pain? Not because they took my burden but because they showed me it was okay to feel. Looking back now, though, I wish my mother had done this with me first; and my grandmother. Emotions weren't okay growing up in my house. Just anger and happiness. Everything else was ignored. And for that reason, I became unable to hold my own emotions until I was forced to as my body imploded with illnesses.

We often think we must fix the pain to make it disappear. But really, the greatest lesson I've learned in knowing the depths of despair itself is that it does not want an exit plan. The tears won't drown you. They are what will help you stay alive the most. Our emotions just want to be seen, held, and honored for being the voice of what couldn't have been spoken aloud.

SINGING DESSERT

I never noticed the sound of birds until I turned thirty-two.

I've always been terrible at listening. The fall after I left Micah, I discovered why.

Stepping into a yoga class at a local studio down the street from my new apartment, the rain clouds beat on with winter creeping closer as the sun left us with less warmth. I knew I needed to move my body to survive winters in the Pacific Northwest. So, despite my fears of the lingering pandemic and the deep breathing in yoga, I decided to try it. I slipped my shoes into a cubby as I arrived at the studio. I found my spot, rolling out my yoga mat in the furthest southeast corner of the room as possible. Wearing my face mask and socks, I tried not to touch too many things, mindful of potential infections that could slow me down to a snail's pace.

The room filled with attendees, each finding their place on their yoga mats. Some began stretching, some took sips from their water bottles, and a few, like myself, scanned the room secretly hoping to meet a new friend. Sadly, no one looked up. Eye contact, the beginning of friendship, seemed to be a lost art these days.

The teacher entered the studio space, checking in the last person who rolled their mat out next to me. As the teacher settled onto her yoga mat at the front of the room, she introduced herself, along with a reason why she might over-explain some poses or adjustments in the vinyasa flow that day. Her explanation became an endearing and helpful story.

As a child, going to the playground was her absolute favorite thing to do. And she'd only be willing to leave if her mother explained precisely why they had to go. She shared a particular story about leaving the playground because dinner would be ready soon, and she'd get dessert afterward. (I think any kid bribed with dessert would agree; yes, now is the time to go.) Yet, her words struck a chord with me—understanding why something happens seems to be a universal desire. If we only know why, we may understand what's happening to us.

Yet, this luxury of understanding was not afforded to me most of my life. I didn't know why I never noticed the sound of birds outside. Why I hated when anyone breathed on me, even though it was never a pungent breath that made me turn sour and want to bolt across the room, as a feeling of snakes wrapping up my legs anchored me to the ground when all I wanted was to grow wings and fly out the nearest window.

A few years before, I left my comfort zone and attended my first Yoga Nidra studio class in my mid-twenties. As I entered the softly lit room, waves of fabric draped across the ceiling as if I were about to sail into the ocean's womb. I found a place next to others who seemed to know what this class was about. The teacher approached me and told me to grab a bolster, two blankets, and two blocks from the back. I set up my space, as I saw others doing, with the yoga mat and folded blankets. I had just finished my Yoga Teacher Training the year before. I knew some poses to put myself into that looked like the others in the room, but this class already seemed different than what I'd learned in my 200-hour teacher training. After the room filled, the teacher welcomed us with a warm smile and gentle voice that promised, "If you've been seeking healing, this practice will change your life."

As I settled onto my mat, my heart raced with excitement and apprehension. The room seemed to cocoon me in the sense of ease. Despite feeling anxious about the illnesses that brought me there, with my handicap sign and the courage it took to leave the house that day, I was always fearful if I'd have the energy to make it back home safely.

We began with gentle yoga flows before the instructor guided us to set up our nests. "We'll be moving into a practice where you must lay as still as possible. Try not to wiggle or itch anything."

I was weary of lying still as my mind swirled with concerning thoughts like, "What if my limbs went numb? Do I lay there?" I slept with compression wear on my arms and legs to keep blood flowing. Without them, I'd wake up to entirely numb limbs, unable to move them as if carrying my dead body. But I followed the instructions, trying to lay my anxieties aside. I closed my eyes, and as the instructor guided us into practice, I felt the tension in my body slowly dissipate.

Yoga Nidra worked its magic, pulling me deep into a restful state. I could feel my heartbeat slowing down, like a soft drumbeat in the background of my mind. My breath became steady and even; gently rocking me like the waves of a tranquil sea, just as the drapes on the ceiling promised. For the first time in years, my body slipped into the most profound sense of safety it had ever known.

Before practicing yoga, I only knew flight: the ability to escape if I pushed hard enough until everything shut off—the ache, the noise, the chatter. I didn't seek pleasure or delight. I sought the death of my voice; the one crying out, "This isn't okay." I silenced it with weary hands, wringing out sound until no drop was left.

It's no wonder I was parched a decade after finding myself wrapped in bed battling chronic illnesses in my twenties. I laid myself in the comforts of bed despite the war within. However, war raged outside with rashes: my skin felt pickled as it curled in, blood red, scabbed, and rugged like the cliff's edge. The one I tried to climb to make everything else go silent—all the pain I experienced under the surface of my seemingly "normal" childhood and subsequent marriage. But instead, I found myself like the cliff, rough and washed from head to toe. Those years in my twenties always brought me back to bed.

After a year of finding this practice, following every online recording I could, and getting trained to teach it, something changed profoundly within me. I finally felt safe in my body. This became my turning point, but it didn't take an expected uphill turn. As Yoga Nidra helped me build new neural pathways in my body and brain, it lit up highways to roads I didn't know I could take. I did not find paradise there, I found a place where only the devil of abuse lived. The one who took all the darkness and tried to swallow me whole. The one who whispered wind on my neck and made my skin tingle. The one who blew fans and made hushed voices repeat, "You're not enough." The one who held the truth of why I didn't receive love with verbal affirmation.

On the healing roads through this meditation practice, I found the key to the sealed door of my subconscious. My brain hid my memories to keep me safe, to allow me to stay present and alive. Along with more nutrient-dense foods, this practice led me to a womb-like room, where I found the darkness and courage to walk through the frame of a pad-locked door painted red with a sign that read, "Enter if you dare." I got close, but instead of opening the locks, ghosts-like memories began to seep out from under the cracks. They wove and swirled around my head, flashing and expanding like the movies, the ones I swore I could never attend.

I felt sick in the movies whenever someone was abused. I couldn't watch them because it made me want to puke. Yet, this time, it wasn't a movie on a black screen casting light, with the promises of make-believe. No. This was my body—my story showing its truth. These things were done to me when no one else looked close.

As the first few memories returned, I asked my sister, Sara, "Do you think anything like this happened to me?"

"No," she replied matter-of-factly. "I was always with you. It didn't." She denied the ghosts. And I think it was then that I never felt like I could trust her as an older sister. She lived in ignorance of what my body knew to be true: this family wasn't safe.

Still haunted by the faint memories resurfacing, I shared with a close friend, Apatha, a trauma survivor herself, working in the DA's office to help people who had faced great suffering find safety and grounding again after getting justice for some of the most horrific things. With her long henna-dyed red hair and tender hands always stained with colors from the hours she spent in her studio releasing all she'd witnessed in this lifetime, Apatha sat with me at my kitchen table. I'd just put Olea to bed, and Micah was in the garage. I told her about my memories.

"I'm not sure if it was me in them."

She cupped her hands on my hand, looked me in the eyes with a long exhale, and said, "What does your body feel?" I wanted to throw up. Those movies I was watching within my subconscious of a little kid getting abused were of me.

In the months and years that followed, more memories and sensations came, and more faces, depth, and life. I began to be afraid of my sleep at night. The phantoms visited me in the first hours of trying to drift to sleep. The phantoms saw me. It was him, my father, and other relatives who were supposed to show me the most safety. My dad always called me beautiful, and now I know why I never believed him. As a child, I turned off his voice. It was no longer declaring any truth.

Their breath on my skin when I barely knew what it was like to be feminine, with voices moaning in my ear telling me, "It's almost over; just be quiet a moment longer. Oh, you like that? I'll do more."

Two years later, nearing the end of my twenties, I began working with a therapist that my friend Apatha recommended. She'd seen it all. She named every ounce of my story and helped me understand the reality of my childhood. It wasn't normal. It wasn't ok. But my body was wise in holding me safe, not to know what happened until I created the safety I wasn't given. These meditations, along with working on eating food straight from the earth gave my body the protection it deeply craved. And with it, I began to hear the song of the birds for the first time.

Then, I learned about my superpower. I didn't notice the noises but the intentions. Compliments don't sink in, nor do the encouragements to make it up that cliff. If you echo it through time and waves, I'll feel your energy more than your sounds. I've learned to read the space more than the consonants. Lavish words do not stick in me as much as words written on a page. I love to linger over them. I want to stand in every space between the letters and wonder why that word?

However, just like the yoga teacher who didn't want to leave the playground, I found my body is my dessert that I trust enough to leave. And now I've given her the voice that was told to hush. With it, she's learning to listen to the songs of the birds but, more importantly, the sound of her own powerful hum.

HONEY CHIPS

After my critique to Olea about how she spoke unkindly to our new blended family because she felt overwhelmed by her unmet needs, she found refuge in the bedroom closet, her long blonde hair draping over her flower-patterned covered knees, as she curled up in a ball. My voice was scratchy from the phlegm in my lungs, a physical manifestation of the perfection that had demanded too much from me as I walked upstairs to console her. I realized that this same pressure of perfection had spilled over onto her like a festering ooze. It made me reflect on the importance of gentleness, a quality we all need in abundance, like water to the clouds.

I opened the door as it scraped on the fluffy rug, and I sat with her. I said, "No one knows your feelings unless you tell them."

As if we could all read minds, she presumed that is what others do when they love you. I imagine her mind exclaiming in thoughts, "But my behavior tells you what I'm feeling, so does my face, my hands, my lips, my entire being! Why don't you understand me?" Yet no sound was uttered. No one truly knows what you are feeling; we can just feel it. This wound many of us hold: wanting to be seen without words. Sadly, we are not that evolved as humans. We can barely read bodies, let alone understand each other's words.

Both Olea and I have a gift for seeing and loving others well, and we've been bred to prioritize their needs. However, it can be isolating when our efforts aren't reciprocated. I wonder if Olea has experienced this herself, not receiving the same level of care in return; or if she has observed me when I was married to her dad.

I would often perceive and react to his needs and emotions. He rarely communicated what he needed. I would overly respond to his perceived discomfort by upending my entire world to pet the feelings of his ruffled fur smooth.

Does she do this with others or expect others to do the same? Sacrificial love and trauma bonding, when witnessed, are the worst poisons I know. I must suck it out now from both of us.

She's wrestling to become older, knowing the realities of the world. Some will love us well, and some barely know how to love themselves. We can choose who we draw near to, even if we can have gentleness towards all. How hard it must be to be so little and full of so much knowledge, so much feeling, with so much sight. With it has come so much tenderness inside of her.

When I opened the door to her closet, I didn't have to prompt or ask it. She knew her words were mean. She already knew in her overwhelm that she replied in frustration instead of gentleness. Oh, how the things we overflow with will always spill everywhere we go. We could ask more often: what am I full of at this moment?

"I'm sorry I was being unkind," Olea said with her face still buried in her knees.

"I'm so proud of you for noticing that, honey. It's one thing to say things unkindly and be unaware of it. But to realize afterwards that your words weren't kind is really important." I offered encouragement.

Awareness works that way. It'll bring light to things we'd usually rather ignore entirely. No matter how much or how little light we place on what we witness and see, the feelings we experience inside will always overflow outside of us. And if we leave them in the dark forever, we'll do so many things we don't recognize as our own; until we look down one day at our hands, at our feet, and in the mirror and wonder, "Who have I become?" In ignoring ourselves, we also deny our very being. So, let's not be afraid of shining the light on what feels terrifying to notice because you deserve to be seen. Every beautiful, unexplainable, mysterious edge of yours deserves to be witnessed and held by your precious, loving hands.

Olea and I continued our conversation, sharing the complex dynamics of becoming an almost nine-year-old. "I know there are a lot of big emotions around you from others every day. And I know, you're experiencing them, too. It can feel like a lot to be around. Still, we must know we're not responsible for other people's emotions or reactions."

"I know," she shot back.

Continuing, I said, "Sometimes still, when I'm overwhelmed or am feeling a lot, I can be unkind in my words, and it's ok. I have to come back and say I'm sorry. Do you recall me doing that to you?"

"Yes."

"And you forgave me, and we moved on. And that's just how it is to be with people. We're all always learning."

I've known so intimately what she's experiencing, too. I don't want to be close to others when they don't want to slow down to see us because they haven't practiced the uncomfortable. It's the beginning of stepping into a world that's asleep when you're already awake, wondering if you want to exist in this dream or create your own reality.

Unknowing exactly how to help her navigate this complex world myself, we did what we could, which was to take responsibility for ourselves.

"Would you like to do our trick with emotions?" I asked her. She nodded her head, now starting to make its way back upright.

As she closed her eyes, I began. "What color is your emotion?"

"Red." She responded quickly.

I proceeded, "What shape is it?"

"Triangle."

"What would you like to do with it?"

"Put it in a jar."

"Ok, beautiful. Where would you like to put this jar?"

"It's full of fireflies now. It says I'm loved."

"That's really beautiful. I'm going to make one like that for me, too. What would you like to do with this jar?"

A smile spread throughout her whole body, she declared, "Dip chips in it and eat it. It's like honey chips!"

We both giggled and remembered we are magicians every single day. But even magicians have to communicate with their audience. So she bravely stepped out of the closet and entered back into her world of becoming the marvelous little girl I'm proud to call my Olea.

BREAKING UP WITH TIME

These phrases constantly ran through my mind: "What time is it? How much time do we have left? Is it already time? How does time get away with us?"

Time. The omnipresent force that shapes our lives, guiding everything with its unwavering tick. I grew weary of the weight it called me to bear. I attributed my deepest wound to the meaning of time: not feeling enough. Every tick, every reminder, manifested my failure.

We're all aboard the wheel, spinning like hamsters. Are we truly moving across the floor, or is it merely an illusion created by centrifugal force?

Time is a shared agreement, an invisible framework we all accept. In our early years, we're blissfully unaware of its grip. Children play until their bellies growl or their little legs tire from adventures in their imaginative worlds. But as they step into the realms of schooling and schedules, caregivers teach them about the existence of time and its boundaries. Gradually, freedom constricts, and a semblance of predictability eases the heart's concerns about the unknowns lurking in the world. Failing to keep up with "the times" is considered disrespectful in adulthood. Yet, it's all merely a product of our collective imagination, similar to the lava monster children pretend to escape from on the playground.

Illusions, constructs, shared agreements, patterns, beliefs: these are the things we label and define, often treating them as modern deities. I wonder how many of us, like those in the past, have placed too much truth in them.

Sitting on a Zoom call in my once shared office with Micah, with my first potential one-on-one business coach, I recall complaining that I never had enough time.

During that phase of my life, I followed a strict healing protocol. Each morning, I would wake up, drink 16 ounces of lemon water, head to the kitchen, and sit on a stool to help from standing for so long. I'd juice 32 ounces of celery, prepare smoothies for Olea and Micah, make my own smoothie, take sixty different tinctures, capsules, and herbal supplements, and then tackle the dishes. My morning routine consumed an hour and a half of my time, which felt like an eternity. I despised it and resented the time it took.

Sometimes, I wondered if I should have simply had a bagel like most Americans; hoping that relinquishing my stress over time spent on nourishment would alleviate my worries. Deep down, I knew I would feel terrible if I abandoned this ritual. The one thing I knew could breathe life into my weary soul was this routine. It allowed me to maintain control over my food choices and let the power of nature heal me.

During that initial coaching session on Zoom, I allowed myself to be seen in my weariness. "John, my morning routine takes an hour and a half. I must take care of my daughter and manage homeschooling by the time I'm done. With my illnesses, I'm exhausted by the afternoon." This amazingly empathetic coach soaked up my grief and reiterated what I needed to be seen in.

"Wow, that is a lot of time." His face expressed with eyebrows raised, and his mouth widened as he spoke.

Days passed, and somehow, waking up at 7 a.m. turned into waking up at 10 a.m., accomplishing nothing except nourishing myself and preparing for the day. A few emails later, amidst a pandemic that trapped us at home, juggling homeschooling while managing the fatigue from my illnesses; I felt drained by noon, having barely touched anything I truly desired.

A shift in perspective occurred simply through the act of being witnessed. Although I couldn't afford to work with that particular business coach at the time, his presence opened up a path to my awakening.

Step by step, I gained more and more support. I began working with a beautiful human, Dr. Chelsea Page, a therapist and coach who landed in my life by sheer destiny. We sat on a phone call together, me first as her branding photographer. As she described her ideal client on the phone, I said, "I think you just described me." We laughed, and then I entered into her world as quickly as she entered mine. Slowly, I digested her lessons about self-care, letting ourselves have desires, and knowing deep love for ourselves. I began to value more and more how much I needed to let go of productivity and embrace caring for myself.

I began to let myself be seen more as well—mostly seeing more of myself. Witnessing the deep grief I'd experienced in life and sitting in self-reflection through regular meditations, writing, and journaling.

I woke up every day when I needed to, for my family, or when my body felt right. I allowed myself to journal through lingering messages from my dreams and slip slowly into my day before juicing celery, taking herbs, and making smoothies. Then, into a yoga flow, where I connected back to the wisdom that my body is constantly communicating, or into a meditation where I let my imagination run wild with messages from my body. It was there in the listening, without the worry of time, I found myself the freest.

I broke up with the guilt of measuring my worth and achievements based on time. I discovered that the restrictions of the clock could never define my value. It became more evident that my self-worth is purely in my existence, not in my ability to nourish myself in a specific way or be as productive as I "think" I need to be in a certain amount of time.

Guilt is so tempting to associate with time. In guilt, there's thoughts like, "I'm late. I haven't done enough. I'm going to miss this."

However, maybe that's just me wanting to throw it up in the air like a wet towel, already too damp from my hair's moisture. I want to run through the warm forest barefoot, splash in the sea, and forever let salt curl the ends of me.

Freedom has no bounds until you tighten her, and she tightens up too much. Often, I feel the restriction of time around my neck becoming a noose. It's these agreements of time that name too much of me.

I hear them call me, "Disrespectful, Sluggish, Slow, Unproductive, Lazy."

In this journey of coming back to myself, unghosting myself, and blooming, I've found that I don't really want to complete any task or achieve any goal, but to feel a certain way: to feel safe, to feel loved, to feel successful, and to feel abundant.

Each day, as I wake up and navigate each moment, I find at any given instant that I can feel anything I want: abundant, successful, safe, loved, held, and worthy. The best part of it all is it's right inside me, inside the wisdom of this beautiful body and my ability to choose.

At any moment, I can close my eyes and ask the wisdom inside of my body to generate these feelings. I can draw in these sensations in my life just through meditation, then through my free will, and actions of choice.

It's there in my depths of loving me, in my being as the creator of my own life, in cherishing each moment and each thing I do, with each person I engage with as if they are the most important thing of that moment. It's there in the being, the really living, that I've found time no longer dictates my worth.

These shared agreements, like time, are just mirrors, as are all within the construct of reality. The mirrors hold up my darkest shadows, asking me, "Will you honor yourself? Will you love yourself like a beloved lover today? Will you believe in yourself to reach for the audacious change you want in the world? Will you let yourself be enough?"

It's simple. I must slip into the robe of self-autonomy. We'll call her Silk and say, "Compassion to you both. Today, we get to decide."

Fill me up with Silk to live in the constructs of time that says: "Yes, I can sleep until noon and be enough." "Yes, I can try not to do too much before I make a plan with you." "Yes, I can forget time as I wrestle with the Lava Monster threatening my playground, whose name I mostly call Shame." "Yes, I can chase those dreams that will change the world."

We deserve both freedom and the truth of remembering. Time is just as made up as the Shame we fear, guilting us to believe we cannot just get lost in play; letting everything beautiful just be.

Nowadays, I'm no longer reaching to accomplish tasks to find my value. I'm no longer trying to achieve anything to prove I'm finally valuable. Instead, I believe I am worthy of all that I deeply desire. Time is just a measurement we made up to give structure, not to measure ourselves.

MONOCHROMATIC

Existence. Living in the present moment happens the most when you feel the life force pulling you deeper. Are you alive? Do you breathe? Can you touch the thread of joy that sends chills up your spine to your lips? It is here I strive to exist. Time was once a relentless taskmaster in my life, a ticking clock that echoed with inadequacy. It served as a ruler, measuring the worth of my every effort. I was like the White Rabbit in Alice in Wonderland, always racing against time. But the Mad Hatter in me knew there was more to existence than this perpetual sprint.

This notion of time as my constant adversary was ever-present during a particular week filled with an array of appointments. I had to go to the DMV after spending a day at Olea's Waldorf school taking photographs, before enduring several hours in a doctor's office for tests. The sterile walls of the doctor's office and the frantic energy at the DMV echoed a relentless ticking of time, carrying the weight of countless uncertainties in my life. The beeping sounds and the squish of crinkling paper on tables inside doctors' offices hold painful memories from a past season when my body started failing to thrive. However, in stark contrast, I experienced the pure magic of my daughter's school, where vibrant colors lined the walls peppered with artwork of all the joys of learning. Laughter filled the stillness between the accumulation of new discoveries and the joyful steps of children; reaffirming my deep desire for her to spend most of her time there. It's fascinating how doctor's and schools dive into the unknown realm, but one often carries tragedy while the other holds the most profound human passion.

Conversely, the DMV is a space brimming with the scope of life; where everyone shows up trying their best, but are mostly filled with exhaustion. I couldn't help but wonder why we don't saturate these places with the same sensory richness we give to art museums. Imagine transforming government offices into spaces we no longer dread but rather places where we become catalysts of paperwork as if we were Willie Wonka filtering chocolate through waterfalls. Sadly, it remains a frustrating environment where everyone does their best to navigate through the lines and shapes we call government.

While at the hospital for lab tests, I head to the room where the tests rely on echoing back formation, akin to the communication of dolphins, with invisible waves traversing through water as it creates mass and shape. The tests were meant to identify shapes that shouldn't be formed. Fortunately, all the results returned negative, both a blessing and a perplexing realization. It's an ongoing mystery of my life with chronic illness, where suffering persists without tangible measurements. I keep wondering whether it is not something within me causing the suffering, but rather all the remembering it's had to hold on to for me.

Triggered by a peculiar memory, as I stepped into the hospital, my body held a whisper that said, "Here is where you'll be cared for." I felt ease, but also grief that this was where my body felt the most care, not my mother's arms, nor my father's arms; not my family or my home. A bridge, long under construction, emerged within me—my pathway to self-care. I recognized that, to move forward, I needed to shift from relying solely on external care to nurturing my inner self. I am trying to make a home within myself, being the one who cares for me the most. Every ounce of attention is to be focused inward, in the most beautiful way, instead of looking outside for constant threats.

However, I negotiated the belief that hospitals are the only places I'll receive care. I reminded myself, "No. The capability to care resides within these bones. I will care for myself."

I recently found myself again in another doctor's office, tending to a part of me that incessantly cried out for attention. These accumulated concerns have been gathering for months, slowly amassing like snow rolled up in a ball. I yearn to listen and remember that I'm constructing a home—a self-care system within me. However, an external part of me insists on ruling out this as nameless, instead of embodied trauma. And so, I found myself in the doctor's office, following the usual pattern of more testing and visits, hoping to reach that familiar conclusion of "we do not know."

When I first fell ill, those words, "we do not know," were repeatedly uttered to me. No one ever knew. All the places that are "supposed to care for you" stood dumbfounded with me. I am the mystery to which their bandaids did not fix.

Walking into a cardiologist's office where my sister had worked during my late twenties, I was at least four decades younger than everyone there. After waiting thirty minutes, Dr. Jantz sat with me on our first visit for over an hour. I've always been happy to wait for doctors who are late because it usually means they are the ones to really sit with you and listen. Of all the doctors I ever worked with, I was so thankful to have more than those who just wrote you a prescription and sent you out of their office.

I brought in a folder as thick as a textbook with test results other doctors had ordered for me, as proof that no one knew what the hell was going on. He looked them over as I explained that I was still passing out when I stood for too long, how exhausted I was despite all the sleep I got, how I was covered in rashes with joints twice their size inside braces. He looked me in the eyes sorrowfully and said, "Well, we've run all the blood work tests we need. Let's get you a Holter monitor to rule out heart conditions."

I returned with the Holter monitor a week later and sat in his office again. Everything was normal, including my heart. "I'm not sure what's going on, but it could be P.O.T.S., a form of Dysautonomia. In the meantime, let's order a Tilt Table Test to rule it out."

A day later, I went to a different floor in the same hospital, exhausted and barely able to drive there while Olea was with Micah's mom. After getting admitted, I was given a wristband in case they had to put me in the hospital upstairs. The nurse checked my blood pressure and asked about my height and weight. Then she strapped me to the tilt table so they could tilt me upright without falling off in case I passed out. She tied on a heart monitor as two other nurses joined in attendance. Then, a doctor walked in. The attending doctor said, "Hi, I'm Dr. McCarty, and I'll monitor your Tilt Table Test. If you have any symptoms, we won't keep you up for long because we don't want to aggravate you so much that you must get admitted to the hospital."

After being fully strapped in and my blood pressure already low, they lifted me slowly to standing. I immediately felt weary. The sinking of gravity pulled me further down to the grave before my time. The room around me started darkening, and I desperately wanted to lie down or move. The interesting thing about my symptoms was that it went away with movement. Standing in lines, or being too still, was most troublesome.

Looking back, I see the terror of being told to be still beneath someone's abuse. Now, a life under the weight of all I felt I had to carry, crushing me to the literal ground.

Quickly, all the alarms went off, my heart rate skyrocketed, and my blood pressure dropped so fast that they had to measure it by hand because the machine could no longer track it that low. They slowly moved the table back, untied me, and everything stabilized itself.

Dr. McCarty declared, "We can call that a positive test result. There's no need to drag it out further. Let us know if you need anything to make it out of the office ok." Her caring eyes lingered with a soft smile, a warmness doctors always want to have to mend the broken.

Deep within, I knew that it is my own attention that I truly need, my own care and affection. Yet, how does one walk when each step brings pain? How does one dance and let go when that pain reverberates through every nerve? I am often thrown into bed, consumed by pain, only to be torn away again by the needs of my flesh and blood as the calling to create and the whirlwind of responsibilities clamor in my head. How can I truly listen when I am caught in the tornado of life?

In moments like these, I yearn to retreat, curl up under the covers, and listen to the whispers within. I have been in that place before, my bed's familiar sanctuary—the most intimate and comforting of homes.

My yellow comforter has held me more than anyone else. I find it ironic that lately, I've dressed like her most days, in shades of yellow. As I donned my yellow sweater and mustard pants, I wondered if part of me needed to take her everywhere.

I have become monochromatic, living in shades of yellow, for I am still learning to see the full spectrum of the rainbow. And perhaps that is why I am drawn to bask in the sunlight, to absorb its energy until being alive feels more like home; until the chills that run up my spine become the very pulse of my existence. I have come a long way, taking each step of every day to reside in a place where this is my life. I will continue to pierce through the veils of uncertainty, remembering that these feet are my own, even if I can only see them when I look down.

As I ascend the stairs to my daughter's classroom, I notice that most people climb without looking down. Yet, I tread cautiously, as if each step holds a secret—a message I must listen to, ensuring that it remains steadfast beneath my weight. It is fascinating how I am still learning to fully trust even the ground I walk upon. So, I, like the students entering this house of discovery, step into more wonder despite all that is still unraveling inside of me. I begin to trust that joy is in staying open to the unknown. It is there in staying curious that I will find more goosebumps daily, filling my cells so much that the old stories cannot haunt me anymore.

TANGLED SHEETS

I used to make my bed like a ritual to remind me I was not my illnesses. I was not my disabilities.

I don't know precisely when the bed-making began. I feel it was about middle school. When I believed the sexual abuse stopped or maybe was the last straw, I ended up medicated, having to lay in my parent's room at night. Something may have shifted then for it to end. Something went in me, too.

I remember being messy when I was younger. My grandma, Julia, was always asking me to pick up my room. She was the one who came over to help my working mom tidy up our house. She always asked me to wipe my perpetually black feet before stepping into the bathtub. I'd stain it with my footprint as if the dirt wanted to tell more stories about where I'd been running around our desert-coated neighborhood. I remember having to tiptoe across my room to reach anything because the floor was filled with curiosity. I got lost in barbies, clothes, endless toys. Growing up, we always got what we desired, so I had every toy a child could ever want. No was rarely a word we heard or one we learned how to speak ourselves.

Yet, something shifted in me. I started to make my bed and clean my room. It became my solace in a world that felt big and chaotic. Even though the illnesses have passed, I still make my bed to this day, and I'm no longer bound to her in fatigue. Part of me needed control when I was at my sickest. But I'm okay with more mess, dirty floors, and feet again today.

But no matter how ill or well I ever was, I always made my bed as if performing a ceremony to remind myself I wouldn't get swallowed alive by her. And we are finally here. This day has arrived. The illnesses are gone, and now she is this sacred reminder of the beautiful tenderness that held me through so much.

Historically, if I nap during the day, I'd often sleep on top of the covers. I think it felt more normal to me. That under the sheets is for the night when it's expected to rest. On top is when you're going gently with yourself. Under all day means you're really sick.

After facing months of not dealing with extreme symptoms, I had to go under the sheets again. Having been ill for over seven years, I've spent more time in bed than I have on my feet. On days when I was the most symptomatic, I felt like she gobbled me whole. But then there was this last time when I felt like I was called to lay with her, reminded of this limiting belief: my worth is not in my doing.

My value doesn't ebb and flow with the sheets floating up and down with the puff of making them.

Yet, recently, after so many days on my feet, running through a forest, and living life having completely forgotten I was ever sick in the first place and once even unable to run, it is all the more painful to find a day when my bed calls me back in. However, now I surrender to the tenderness and thank her for all the beautiful truths she helped me release, every trauma healed, every symptom given a voice, and all the beautiful words she helped me pen out declaring to myself and the entire world, this reality that says "you are forever sick" isn't one you have to accept.

I find it ironic, my Moon, my beloved husband, refuses tucked-in sheets. Each night with him, the sheets become tumbled, twisted, turned, and well-lived in. Yet, with his untucking, I've found the most home, the release to the beliefs that we all don't need to pretend to have it together and lay uncomfortably on what's already been made. We can get under. We can get dirty. We can get messy because we deserve to live.

My bed, she's become this womb, where my body gets to go do its most profound work of becoming me. I must remember this truth and rewrite it as I relearn it's okay to have a messy bed and dirty feet that have stories to tell.

SPACE TO BE

"I need to be alone," I admitted as my voice ladened with weariness. Depression crept up on me as the evening came along.

"But Mommy, I haven't spent much time with you today," my daughter's innocent plea tugged at my heart, as we now only have half of our time together after the divorce from her dad.

"Let's hug for a moment and make dinner together," I suggested, attempting to bridge the gap between my need for solitude and her desire for connection.

As we pulled out a pumpkin muffin box and began to mix, I chuckled at the idea that tonight, we'd be dining on muffins and peas, the hallmark of single mothers who avoid fast food. I texted Moon, who was driving home after a twelve-hour journey across three states with his two young girls. His messages conveyed the beauty of the sunset before him, mentioning uncertainty about getting groceries that night or the next day due to their empty cupboards. My desire to care for him led to an offer to go grocery shopping on his behalf. I texted, "I'm serious. What do you need? I'll go and get your supplies."

I realized that my willingness to overlook my own needs for his sake was a familiar pattern. It's a way to cope with grief, but it won't heal the underlying wounds that only our hands can mend. His response was simple and firm. "No, I'm good."

I felt a motherly response boiling over. "Why are you so stubborn?" But what came out of me was a response as sharp as a freshly razored knife. "One day, you'll let me do things for you."

Slice the throat—that's the quickest way to bleed. Passive-aggressive, just like he had told me was his childhood wounds. I crumbled the muffins I was baking. Squished with an aggressive hand too hungry, finding less actually hit my mouth than the floor, where it's now a disaster scattered with cinnamon sugar. Sweet and sticky mixed with bare feet, it was all the good put on the wrong part.

I realized my error and sweetly replied, just like I tried to sugar my foot, "I'm sorry, please erase that. I don't mean it. You let me do things for you all the time."

Everything scrunched like ponytail holders around my face. I audaciously noticed, "Did I just say to my love, why won't you let me love you how I want to?" As if, like my abuser, I was supposed to find pleasure in the ways he stole my body.

He sweetly replied, "Groceries are not a love language of mine."

My mistake made me ponder. Am I projecting my desires onto him? Internally, I asked myself, "Do I not love myself in the ways I want to be loved?" Despite my daughter's wish to play a card game, I asked her, "Can you listen to some music while I take a moment alone?" She climbed into her bed, and I laid down with a pillow over my head, wondering if I could be loved how I desired. So often, I've felt the pressure to love myself and receive love in prescribed ways. As the first man who was supposed to teach me love, my abusive father, sent me this message. "Oh, you like this too? This is love, me taking from you and making you feel things you don't even know yet. Oh, do more of that? I like that. You like it messy, don't you, with that extra jelly on your PB&J bread." Unable to play with my daughter because of the poison spread in my root, I'm ragging with grief. Is this why so many want to be alone? Why are there so many couples who are distracted instead of interacting? Is this why we yell at our kids because we hold so much pain? With triggers that light the fire, we're so detached we don't know what set off the flame.

I'm not a wildfire anymore. I can see where my fuse gets set off. But I have to dive in quickly before I lose it. I let out a spark to Moon when I felt this pain. I don't want to spitfire anymore. Will this get easier? Will there be fewer strings coated with pyrotechnics visco green? I'm tired of not being able to mommy or live an intimate life in my relationships because of the sea of bombs that may detonate, forcing me to step through carefully. Something will trigger it, and then it feels like my entire life will be disrupted. This is the reality of having PTSD.

Can you tell me, my dear, what it's like not to be afraid with every step you take?

I sat next to my dear friend, Lindsay, in the car on our way to the Green Sand Beach during our trip to Hawaii with Olea to celebrate my divorce. She was calm, and I was anxious. I've only known scarcity, and she's lived in abundance. I massaged her shoulders that morning in a yoga class I led for her and two other men staying at the same community lodge. We'd spent the night and morning connecting and talking, and I was eager to share my gifts. As I massaged Lindsay, I wondered what it's like not to carry the trauma I've had.

Maybe my shoulders wouldn't be hunched up to my ears. Perhaps my belly would be flat. Could I believe that everything will be okay? I'm grateful for beautiful souls like hers so that my biology can learn, just by witnessing—this can also be the calm in which you could exist in. It's possible to leap past generational traumas and embody new nervous systems.

I know this is my work: to not pass on any more of this trauma to my daughter. But damn, I was tired of missing so much of her childhood because I had to take space just to be.

Feeling trapped in the unknown, I asked myself, "Do I even love to be cherished like I have been? Do I want to be held? Do I want any of this?"

I heard the line from The Notebook, as Noah shouts to Ally in their day-old clothes after they rekindled their love from years past when she was about to marry someone else, "What do you want?"

She wept. "It's not that simple."

He replied sternly. "God damn it. What do you want?"

Turning her head away, then down, she said, "I have to go," pulling away in her car.

Yet, I'm wondering if that is my story, too. Needing to rid myself of this poison before becoming the woman I wanted to be, enough for my new partner and myself. Or was it the fear that he'll leave once he found out I'm too much? Or really was it that I believed I'd go, again and again, as I found how much I still had left—a lingering trauma string around my neck.

But as I sat weeping into my pillow, clutching my blanket, I knew no one could rescue me. I wanted to call Micah to take Olea because I dove too deep. Hitting an edge where the neuropathway of suicide slipped in, it's like I wanted to dive right off the cliff. The one where death tastes like the juice of a pomegranate after I'd just cut my lip as I tried to swallow the mirror of the wounds I was told to digest.

In reality, I needed to release these emotions to let them flow into love.

Feeling paralyzed, and unable to ask for help, haunted by the fear that I would leave a legacy of trauma for Olea, I turned to meditation. In my mind's eye, I saw the woman I wanted to become. She exuded a soothing presence and reminded me of the progress I had made. My thoughts wandered to a café on the cliffs of Greece. She spoke, "I know you're hurting. But look how far you've come. You're just beginning. It's all coming. We're here, you just can't see it."

She spread her arms wide, reminding me of everything I've overcome.

"You're in the room with all the friends you dreamed of. You're healing your body from the ones that told you there was no cure. You went roller skating with your daughter after you went sledding. You just went to Hawaii by yourselves, not on anyone else's dime but your own! You traveled with a close friend. You're not stuck in bed covered with rashes wanting to die. You've made it so far. You drive every day. You don't need that wheelchair. You've left the marriage that was only hurting you. Look at the glorious place you live in now. You make your own money. My dear, this is just the beginning. Look how far you've come in just these past ten years. Wait until it's been twenty."

I stayed curled up in my ball and began to open myself a bit more as I saw myself there, too, with the ocean below us in the cafe I'd been dreaming about with the writer who gets paid to travel to these marvelous places. I asked if we were alone.

She smiled at me and sweetly whispered, "Oh no. Of course he's here. He's just gone to get us drinks."

Opening my eyes and returning to reality, I heard Olea shifting on her bunk bed across from me in our 300-square-foot apartment. I embraced this pause, nourishing my soul and affirming that I deserved love. I didn't have to be alone indefinitely due to my PTSD. I could take the space I needed to defuse the emotional landmines in my heart. Many will be set off, and each one deserves grace. In these moments, I made a pact with myself: to learn to listen to my needs and prioritize them, allowing me to love more freely in every aspect of my life.

Peering through Olea's curtains, which divided her room in our studio apartment, I asked her, "Do you want to come down and read with me before getting ready for bed?"

With her pink headphones on, she smiled and nodded at me. She turned off her iPad and came down to join me on my bed. We cuddled for the rest of the evening as we learned about monkeys with worldwide explorers.

Although I fear resentment can accumulate due to the amount

of space I occasionally need, I'm thankful that the people in my life don't always require me to prioritize their needs over mine. This societal belief often burdens mothers and women in relationships. We deserve separation so we can tunnel under the comforts of pillows to heal the pieces of us that were told they don't belong.

MUASHA

Laying on my bed, I waited for Olea to finish brushing her teeth to join me for snuggles before going to sleep. We now live with Moon and his two daughters, Jean and Maddie, in a little two-bedroom condo. Jean walked into my bedroom with blue and white tie-dyed workout pants pulled up really high on their belly. With a gray sports bra on, they squeezed the top of their chest to their belly, and the flesh puddled out over the lip of the pants. They exclaimed, like they'd just discovered the most beautiful piece of art, "Look at my Mausha!"

Beauty culture, being so ingrained in me, wanted to correct them and say, "Oh no, honey. That is a muffin top." Instead, I tried to add some quip about it being funny, even though my mind constantly critiques the extra layers from the top of my own pants.

By the divine miracle of practicing letting my soul speak more, I instead turned, using the trick we always have in every moment of life, and said, "Will you show me how to have one too?"

They said, "Yes! You'll need a sports bra and high pants." So I lifted up my shirt, pulled up my layered wool pants, squished my chest to my belly, and said, "Muasha."

We all giggled, as I thought in hidden tears, "If only we all reinvented what it meant to be human instead of letting anyone else tell us how we should be shaped or formed."

What if thunder thighs could become power peddlers? Or even better, what if back fat bulging over bra straps could become angel wings? Or butt cheeks hanging out of underwear, Squishacush?

We often think we're teaching our children, but it's always the other way around. That is the greatest gift of parenthood. Witnessing these fantastic souls share their wisdom. I'll hold them dearly and encourage them never to stop sharing what they feel is true, what they know as beautiful, and how to make a new name for this part of their human dwelling.

COVER GIRL

My dad used to call me beautiful and gorgeous, but I never really believed him. This could be a common thing for most girls growing up. But perhaps it was more because my body couldn't trust his words after he had stolen from it too many times before. It's something my brain had forgotten over time, only to have my body remind me in my thirties, as I finally began to heal.

I experimented with makeup during my younger years, going through the glitter and ribbons phase in middle school. I once spent an hour pinning golden ribbons to the top of my scalp, hoping to feel a little bit more marvelous on the days we had to all dress alike in our khakis and polo T-shirts. However, the desire to wake up an hour earlier for school quickly wore off. I decided that if anyone found me beautiful, it would have to just be me, not how sparkly I could become with all that extra glitter. So, I stopped wearing makeup.

On a first date at the small Christian college I briefly attended in rural Tennessee, I followed suit. I wore makeup like all the other girls. Although my time there was short, due to the extreme cultural shock of growing up in the Rocky Mountains in a more liberal, bigger city, it was the one time I felt like I fit into this culture: being out on a date with a sweet southern boy all dolled up.

All the other girls would wake up hours before class to put on makeup, do their hair, and become "presentable." I found it quintessential that, just like girls in a movie, they would go through all their clothes, tossing them all over our dorm to find the perfect outfit just to look a certain way. I had grown accustomed to sleeping in and rolling out of bed, maybe brushing my hair, and at the least, wearing an outfit I felt good in. Spending hours in front of a mirror was unfamiliar to me.

I remember feeling out of my element when I decided to wear makeup on that first date. My roommates were so excited for me to have my first official date as a college girl. All four gathered in my room to help me pick out my white polka-dotted dress that had a peach bow around the rib cage with trim at the bottom. I curled my hair and wore makeup for one of the first times in college.

On a late afternoon, we met at a local ice cream shop just a short walk from my dorm room. After getting our ice cream, we sat by a window. I mentioned how uncomfortable I felt with all this makeup on. "I usually don't wear this much makeup. It feels so heavy and exhausting to do all the time." "You look really nice. You know, my mom wears something called Bare Minerals. She says it's like wearing nothing at all," he sweetly offered.

This got me wondering about the concept of women and makeup. Was it to conform to what everyone else was doing? Or was it because society told us we needed to be something other than ourselves?

Then, later in life, there was Micah. He strongly disliked makeup on me, often referring to it as the "cake in the face." This was a term from our high school theater days when stage makeup was literally caked onto our faces. He said it made my eyes look droopy. Yet, he rarely called me beautiful. In fact, I think he spoke it more times to another girl he tried to fuck, than he said it to me. But hey, maybe that's just my post-divorce anger speaking for a hot sec. Facts of the memory are rarely reliable, but the emotions we feel are one hundred percent correct.

After Micah's betrayal, I felt beautiful for the first time during my therapy session. We sat in a corner office on the third floor of a business complex twenty minutes away from Micah and I's second apartment on the outskirts of Denver. My therapist, Kathy, with ringlet curls tucked neatly in a ponytail, sat in her soft brown chair across from me. Books were stacked on a shelf behind her, and a sound machine drowned out noise so no one else could hear our conversation.

She asked me, "What makes you feel beautiful?"

Pausing momentarily on the couch next to a lamp and a tissue box, I replied, "Dancing makes me feel beautiful. I used to dance in middle school and high school. I was even a part of the student company and choreographed pieces for my high school theater productions."

"You should do more of that." My therapist smiled in full reply.

So I did. I enrolled in an adult ballet class at the Colorado Ballet Academy. The first few classes felt extremely rusty, not having danced for four years through college, as well as my first few years of being married to Micah because we couldn't afford for me to take classes. But a few years later, my photography business was doing well, and I could take at least one class a week.

Walking into the studio with my old tights and high school leotard on, I returned to those moments when everything went silent. My body and I were one. This was my time to speak everything my voice wasn't strong enough to express.

When I first started dancing in middle school, my teacher quickly bumped me up to a higher level because she said she saw something in my dancing that she didn't see in many other students.

After only being in an introductory ballet class for six months, I went to the higher level classes. Having been a gymnast throughout my whole childhood, I felt very lost in all the terminology. I felt out of my own world, surrounded by girls who'd been dancing and learning this lingo since they were five. After the class, Celcia pulled me aside next to her mixtapes and corner speakers across from the mirror, and said, "I know this is a lot, but the first time I saw you perform for the recital, I saw something that most dancers only dream of experiencing. Your expression had my eyes fixated on you the whole time. It was hard to notice the other dancers."

Being fourteen, I didn't know what to do with this, but I let it fuel my desire to keep dancing because it was something I didn't understand but was madly in love with.

Every time I danced, I felt beauty tingle through my bones and come to find its home in my blood. It really wasn't about seeking validation from others. It was about movement through song and emotion, transmuted to energy for the adoration of the one expressing and perhaps the one watching. It was self-generated; an expression of my authentic self, the one often told didn't exist, or the one that needed to be quiet. Dancing was the place where I could finally tell my truth safely.

As I grew older, makeup became another form of self-expression I refused to participate in. Without succumbing to society's pressure to plaster my face with colors and shapes, I forged my path. Serums, soaps, paints, and brushes remained foreign to me. I wore makeup for my wedding with Micah, but beyond that, it was minimal.

Recently, as a newly divorced adult and mother to a seven-year-old girl about to get interested in makeup, I was curious. What would it be like if I adorned myself entirely? I stepped into my bathroom and stared in the mirror longer than usual. (I rarely even do my hair.) I lifted the lashes with that long, fuzzy eyelash brush and turned my eyes just a little bit wider. I pulled out the forgotten container of powder and paint brushes only known for a human canvas and began to play. Hilariously enough, I found old Bare Minerals makeup from when I married Micah. As I was taught, I stroked on the brush with extended sweeping circles inside the powder, tapped it on the side, and then added a little darkness to the cheeks. As I painted, I heard a voice inside me saying, "Blend in those dark red spots."

As I applied the makeup, I noticed things I hadn't before: the dark spot on my chin, the dry patch on my brow, and the darkness under my eyes.

Was this why women hate themselves? Because they stepped too close? Do they just begin to pick apart all that isn't smooth, taut, and imperfect; judging it harshly and wishing for it to disappear? Yet, as a photographer and artist myself, I know that sometimes, when you look at something too closely, you miss the beauty of everything together. And I think this is the tragedy all humans face when stepping too close.

After a bit, I was all painted up. My face felt heavy, and I felt lost. Yet, in some denial, I wondered if this is what beauty is supposed to look like—the girl, all covered up.

The unknown voice echoed in my head, "Did you bring yours? Maybe it's there that we'll find beauty drenched in fake sand?"

I grabbed my camera and played in the light coming through my apartment window to see what I had discovered. Did I feel like the dame I wished to find, the one who felt like a goddess, desired, and lavished?

Instead, I felt weighted down. I felt like a prisoner thrown into a tunnel with the door sealed shut.

After a while, I got tired of feeling so weighted and misplaced. So, I ran to the bathroom, removing the makeup with a damp cloth and regular soap. The sensation of liberation was profound. Sigh. A deep breath finally caught in my lungs.

I approached the same mirror, camera in hand, exploring angles and light. I felt even more. Stripping off my shirt, I examined a body that had recently not felt like home. More shapes have come to adorn it. Although, honestly, they've felt more like aliens than decorations. But I'm trying to find a home for them, too.

Nothing felt quite right. I didn't feel beautiful. So I stripped off my pants, set up my camera timer, and focused on my bed. I let my body move in the ways it wanted to express.

Oh! Oh! Did I discover it here? Raw, naked, with nothing pressing in on me, where I finally felt beautiful?

I felt powerful.

I felt alive and sexy as hell.

I saw what my lover saw—the shapes, curves, shadows, and light. I acknowledged areas I was uncomfortable with, realizing that perspective can distort reality, just as a misaligned brush can alter a painting. I shifted my focus to the angles that felt more like summer garlands, embracing the changing form.

I wanted to find beauty, and I did, right here with nothing on. Naked, raw, loving every dancing shadow and shape.

However, what struck me the most was this aching thought at how many women haven't known the feeling of their own raw beauty because they've been told they need to be a cover girl.

AN APOLOGY TO CUTE

Salty drip-kissed cheeks bear an apology to the girl I believed I should become. "Be interested in the things they like," they told me. "And maybe then they'll notice you." "Dress like them, blend in." The unspoken rules continued, advising me to keep those hundred ribbons out of my hair to stifle my natural quirks, to silence my mind, and to take up the hobbies that they found appealing. It worked just like I knew it would. I met my first boyfriend after I had turned my body that was becoming a woman into a shape more like a boy, invisible until I turned sideways. Band t-shirts and jeans became my uniform, and I could be found at concerts every late Friday night.

I fell in love with music, but as I squeezed myself into skinny jeans and shirts I'd sewn to fit even tighter, I squeezed out the femininity within that had always longed to twirl on stage in glittering gowns.

Throughout my life, I found myself continually becoming something or someone to earn the attention of others.

But it was never enough. So I mastered the most exceptional trick of Homo sapiens: adaptation. A chameleon of extraordinary ability, I could be the band girl crowd-surfing on Friday nights to catch every boy's attention, the good Christian girl on Wednesday nights to curry favor with my mother and grandmother, and the diligent student to secure my father's approval. The only thing I ever did purely for myself was dance.

I did get to choose French over Spanish. Still, my life was shaped very early on by the imperative to become the version of myself that could most effectively attract the attention I so deeply craved.

I became the ideal picture for my ex-husband until he discovered that this wasn't honestly me. Perhaps I never truly became myself until my body decided it could no longer play this role. It froze in time until it had nothing left but to defrost. And I finally remembered my love for running barefoot, for being watched and adored by my grandmother in her kitchen, and for telling stories; particularly those about how many cookies I managed to snatch from my aunt Margot's cookie drawer.

There was always one in my hand and another stuffed in my cheek. Margot, leaning in as adults do with children, would ask, "That's your second cookie, isn't it?" She knew I would nod with a mouth full of what was also my "second" one. We'd both pretend. I wonder how many other secrets she kept, thinking they were cute but perhaps not the best.

I would flutter my eyes, the eyes my family would refer to as my "pretty eyes." Using this endearing deception to cover up my little lies. How often do we attempt the same kind of manipulation with our bodies, declaring with dramatic charm, "My dear, it's cute! We can do things we don't like." I said the same to my teenage self, gazing into the mirror as I squeezed myself into those band t-shirts and skinny jeans.

Though I still own a few of these shirts, alongside yoga pants, which are essentially just skinny jeans with more patterns and colors, I'd much rather twirl in a dress, barefoot on the sand, with my beloved's eyes locked on me.

I'm still untangling the idea of "cute" because now I demand the kind of beauty that stops your breath and leaves you in awe.
This truth has the power to transform your heart forever and remind you that you are worth more than just "cute." You are a creation of exquisite beauty, recognized in all you touch and experience. Promise me you will never forget this because stuffed cheeks will always surpass the idea that you should be compressed into a "two"?

I promise you, it's true. Just ask your eight-year-old self; they hold all the secrets you've been forced to squish out.

LAVISHING BEHIND CLOSED DOORS

Have you noticed you can only offer yourself love after you've found your place in this world by helping others? These quiet whispers of your heart rarely have a voice because you feel you haven't served enough.

This profound realization crashed over me like relentless waves meeting unyielding cliffs. Its impact resonated as water playfully splashed against my fingertips in the kitchen sink.

Each day, the pain seemingly grows larger inside my body, the pain that has been with me for seven long years. Some days, it's blissfully empty. Some days, it roars so vehemently that all I can do is listen while absorbed in its anguished cries.

One day, its voice emerged gentler—a plea simply to be heard. Yet, I'm in this paradox because finally, after months and months of feeling stuck inside a lost tunnel of knowing I have so much to offer, but unable to trust it all to come together, I saw the glimmering light at the end and began racing towards it. However, I looked down and saw I had already given too much of myself.

I'm still recovering from oversharing out of my own deficit of trying to feel valuable. I heard my soul speak to me at that moment, reminding me, "You cannot keep trying to help people when you are still the patient in the hospital bed."

Those of us who have been taught to embody through examples from abuse and inherited lies, that our best use is in serving others, often find ourselves in agony. We ache. We burn with a fierce intensity. Our bodies echo the truth we've been too blind to see. We reach outwards, seeking validation from the external. Our inner turmoil manifests as pain, demanding our attention, desperate to remind us that we are absolutely worthy of our own divine love, of embracing the truth encoded in our stardust DNA. This truth beckons us to step into an embodied remembrance of the full spectrum of love constantly whispering to us to return home.

Stepping away from the kitchen sink after this awakening, I settle onto my yoga mat, my joints voicing their call to remember. As the flickering sun dances in and out of the clouds, reaching through my window to touch my skin, I stretch my body and create space to open, listen, and give voice and movement.

I want to love every sacred ounce, whispering, "You have all my love, all my attention. I'm right here for you, lavishing you." Yet, the mind of a yoga teacher kicks in; the desire to share this newfound wisdom, to craft a class allowing others to touch this experience. And while my excitement to share is similar to a child who just "discovered the most beautiful rock they've ever seen and must show you right now." It also holds this wound that I cannot truly love myself until I can be deemed valuable enough for you to see me share my truth.

Raindrops fall, not from the sky, but from within, caressing my cheeks, mirroring the grief I bear. It's me I need to make all this for. It's me I need to keep witnessing, loving, and lavishing; because it's for her: the little girl in me who was not loved for being herself but for what she could do and how she could perform for others. It's her I'm rescuing. It's her I'm going to choose today for.

So, while every ounce of my being yearns to dive into the ocean of beautiful ideas coursing through me, I'm committing to actions that resonate with worthiness, that amplify love for her—the one who deserves it most.

It will look like dressing powerfully on days like this, wrapping myself in clothes that draw out my confidence. It will look like nourishing myself with colorful foods, savoring every bite, and filling my body with the energy it deserves. It will look like I am finally working on some projects just for me. Projects that reflect my passions and dreams without the need for external validation. It will look like letting myself get silly with my new family, married to Moon. We'll dance our hearts out in the living room and let our bodies express unbridled joy. It will look like snuggling my husband for hours, feeling his warmth and strength as I'm reminded, "I belong." It will look like nothing "important," which is the very point.

Sometimes, our best form of self-love is where we do things when no one is watching and no one is noticing. It's the holy act that we get to whisper to ourselves each time we stand in front of the mirror and relearn how to adore ourselves in a way only true lovers do. These whispers weave themselves in consecrated corners, beneath sheets, behind closed doors: where you are seen most intimately and purely. And as you emerge, you're absolutely glowing. It's this sacred secret between you and yourself that you, darling, are your own damn beautiful lover. Go love her, just like that.

HARMONY

YOU DESERVE
TO BELONG

YOU ARE WORTHY OF YOUR SOUL'S DESIRES

CLEVER SWEATERS

We sat on our monthly Zoom call inside my coach's program, The Naked Experience. Inside our two little boxes, I lived on my bed, cozied with my laptop and a blanket. At the same time, she sat in her office three states away in Colorado. Her blonde curls framed her soft and loving face.

We've spent over two years together, taking us eighteen of those months to realize why I started to get sick when Micah began sharing more and more about why he didn't want to be married.

"I am beginning to put together this realization. When I was little, my whole family would dedicate so much of their time and attention to my cousin when she got cancer again after having already had it four times. It was the attention I deeply craved from them, but rarely felt like I received."

"Wow, your inner safety mechanism is clever to tap into people's compassion to receive the love you need."

Our conversation continued, but after our meeting, I realized that I didn't get sick when I was little but I did when I was married to Micah.

We loved our alone time. Micah had his creative pursuits after work as a singer-songwriter, spending the first year of our marriage at work or with his best friend, having late nights recording in the attic of his office. Meanwhile, I kept myself occupied with rock climbing or out on photoshoots for work. However, most of our eleven-year-long relationship was marked by a constant push and pull of rejection. He came back to me often saying he wasn't sure if he wanted to be married.

The first conversation began when we were dating. Sitting at Frontier, a local cafe in our hometown; with french fries, their quintessential cinnamon buns the size of your face, him with coffee in a porcelain mug, and me with water in an opaque plastic cup. We'd been dating for nine months. His long brown hair slid down his face, the veins on his hands bulging on his fingers. As he rubbed his rounded chin, he told me, "I'm not sure I want to keep dating."

"Why? We seem to be doing really well. Tell me you aren't enjoying yourself or why, and I'll gladly say goodbye, too."

He never had an answer, and I was good at reminding him why I was the perfect fit for him. So we kept staying together, not knowing what we were doing as two kids who were nearly twenty.

A month later, in his room in a shared house where he lived, we laid snuggling on his couch as a Nag Champa incense burned next to us and Iron and Wine played on the record player near our feet. Snuggling in close, he said, "I want to marry you."

Everything in me hit my belly in some sort of roller coaster g-force and had me reply, "Really?" When a deep part of me wanted to scream, "Why?"

This pattern of him wanting to leave but drawing me closer repeatedly continued for the next eleven years. In desperation, I sincerely believed that this was going to work out. But I realized it goes beyond simply wanting someone's attention or seeking to feel special, appreciated, and loved. It's deeper than that. Giving my full attention to making someone who is feeling so sad feel good was the only way

I knew how to receive love and find a sense of safety.

I have faint memories of late elementary school when I fell ill with an infection that required me to sleep on my parents' floor. Blankets were layered on each other, and my pillow moved to the floor next to my mom's side of the bed and their bathroom door. I remember waking up every few hours to take medication, but I do not remember what for. However, it was during this time that the abuse seemed to stop. When my body experienced illness and harm caused by others, it found a means to meet its needs.

Sincerely longing to break free from suffering and illnesses, I had been grappling with what was at the heart of my illnesses. I now give myself the loving attention I need, the love that I used to ache for from Micah. I care for myself daily with tenderness and gentleness in the ways my parents couldn't provide. The urge to push me beyond my limits, like the sexual abuse taught me, has diminished. The need to work until I have nothing left has been replaced by a call to prioritize the ease and alignment of my heart, even when I feel lost. I continue to take small steps in the direction that feels right. Many people credit me with being attuned to my body. I'm thankful I can serve as a witness for others to do the same.

Now, I long for these illnesses to come to an end. Every morning, I wake up exhausted. I experience joint pain that swells my limbs, nausea triggered by many foods, debilitating period pain that confines me to bed for two days each month, and jaw and neck pain that radiates, even when closing my eyes at times. It all screams for me to turn inward. The infections persist, and the remnants of my womb crumbles, scraping the surface as if it never could hold life. There's an unnamed pain in my core, blood samples come back clean from other tests, anxiety cripples my every step, and depression often beckons me to step into oncoming traffic. The list seems endless. I've been through divorce before, and now I want it again, from all the symptoms.

So, I go into the wisdom of my body in meditation. I sweep through my living room, music in my ears, my home empty, a soft rug beneath my feet, and this practice I've been cultivating for years. I'm determined to heal." This is the end! I am breaking up with suffering! I am breaking up with you, illnesses! We are not victims. We are creators!" I declared as a deep base pulsed through my ears. Tears streamed down my face as if I were addressing an audience of my cells—my past, present, and future selves. They were listening, but they didn't shift.

I found myself puddled on the red carpet floor, curled back into the ball I always find myself in. Heartbreak consumed me, much like a lover who promises not to hurt me despite the constant lies they tell. "When will you listen?" I want to shout at my cells, knowing they are doing their best. Every day I survive, I endure.

After divorcing Micah, I touched a place of promise within myself. I felt liberated from illness, free from the toxic marriage that had plagued me for a decade. I discovered that I have the power to create the life I truly want. I became like a fairy spirit, experiencing joy daily and effortlessly flowing through life as if my skin were not scared from within. The intoxicating high I experienced resulted from my wonder and the realization that everything I desired was within my reach.

I had finally generated enough income to move out of the shared home with Micah, ask for a divorce, and move into my own place to share half-time with Olea. I began following my desires for a life with a man I adored. I spent months dreaming of him but realized I kept trying to believe Micah could be him, this sweet, thoughtful, playful man I wanted my partner to be one day.

Until Moon came to me in this season. We met and began a whole new chapter of life together. The illnesses started to heal, and I could travel alone for the first time in five years, work without getting exhausted, and take care of Olea alone.

However, suddenly, as if the devil had crawled into my bed, all the wellness slipped away. A sudden breeze stripped off my wings, and I could not take flight. The illnesses returned just as fast as they seemed to disappear.

How curious it is to personify the truth of trauma as a devil, as if externalizing it allows us to confront it better and understand it. But the true power lies in integrating all the darkness within us, finding a way to transform the horrendous into something beautiful. We are wise beings, masterful magicians, and cunning creatures.

Unraveling layer by layer, I realized that the fairy spirit I had become was nothing more than a dream, a promise from the universe that said, "This is your truth, but now you must face your demons."

So here I am, staring them straight in the eye. I see now that illness, a demon that has plagued me, served to teach me about love and keep me safe. When I became sick, the abuse stopped. The illness became a shield, protecting me from further harm. It prevented Micah from leaving me as well. He would never abandon his chronically ill wife. Only when I stepped out of the realm of illness, just enough to realize I could survive without him and create my own safety, did I finally find the courage to ask for a divorce.

But the funny thing about old habits is that they try to cling to you, like a favorite sweater you've outgrown, yet you still cuddle with it in bed. Somehow, its sleeves still wrap around your arms, and you engage in behaviors you no longer desire.

Illness does the same thing. However, I now understand that illnesses are merely messengers, reminding me of everything I have yet to learn to give myself. Safety is one of those things I have had to know without a coping mechanism. So, to wish illness away is to ask me to step into chaos again. But all good teachers must conclude their lessons once the student has grasped them.

I see these lessons now, and now is my time to embark on a journey of remembrance, to recall what my soul already knows: I create my own safety. I am the embodiment of love. And belonging resides within my connection with myself and my compassion for others. I am simply enough because I exist. I will carry these clever sweaters with me until I can look down and finally see my own skin as the most cherished and beloved garment I possess.

DEFROST

Kelly was my first friend who was a therapist. She had the openness and depth to her as all good friends do. The ones that slow down to actually listen to your heart. They offer only solutions if you ask and help you know how to hold yourself well, as they show you first.

We sat on her bed during a church small group meeting. Every Wednesday night, we'd gather in a small group of people who went to our church in northern Denver to get together for a bible study and share what we're going through in life. After our bible study, the men and women would split into two groups for more focused time. The men would stay downstairs in their living room. At the same time, the women went to their bedroom for privacy and cozied around each other. Kelly's bed was always full of plush pillows, decorated with a clean style, while still making you feel like you could climb on the bed and it wouldn't be a big deal if you messed up the covers.

Kelly shared an image one night, "This is true empathy."

It was an image of a character personified as Sad with a box of tissues inside a dark hole. The four squares, in the style of a comic book, showed a character stepping down a ladder. The characters entered the same spot and sat with the stick figure wrapping their arms around them. No words were exchanged, just pure empathy.

That simple comic has never left my head.

As I battled chronic illnesses, empathy had to become my life. One I followed, one I'm forever grateful for, but one that would never allow numbness or distraction to take over my life.

Although, I wonder if this attribute is more of who I am more than anything, not wanting to settle for what I've been told, but wanting to experience everything once I have my heart set on it. I tenaciously reach for what I want.

When I was sixteen, my aunt Talia enrolled me and my cousin Teal in a snowboarding class. The instructors had us line up to take turns to fall more times than slide down the hill. Meanwhile, my aunt was teaching my mom and sister Sara how to ski. As she descended the green slope, passing us for the fourth time, she jokingly shouted at me, "You should trade that board in for skis!"

The class was marketed as "guaranteed to snowboard" by the end of the week. However, by day three, I caught the snowboard's edge, and my body catapulted four times over itself, along with the snowboard attached to my feet. Surprisingly, only my arm was complaining of pain. The instructor and medical staff soon arrived, pulling me down on a sled to the medical building. They examined my arm and announced there was no break, but it was probably severely bruised. So, I sat in the cabin for the rest of the trip while my family finished their adventures.

Determined to figure this out, my aunt's questioning of my ability to master snowboarding only drove me further to succeed. The next time I visited a ski hill, I had a different teacher. This time, he taught me another way, but the most important thing was that I didn't give up. When my aunt told me I should call it quits, I shouted back, "I'm going to figure this out!" After five years of trying to learn, everything finally clicked.

I've always been stubbornly tenacious. It has served me well all my life, but it wasn't until I had genuinely learned empathy that it became helpful. Tenacity can force you to push yourself too hard without regard for your feelings. I had to realize I deserved happiness and that sacrificing pieces of myself to get what I wanted does not have to be the script of my life.

Before I knew empathy, I did have my coping mechanisms to attempt to satisfy my ever-boiling emotions. While I never battled with addictions or the typical recreational curiosities of most people, food had always been my source of comfort, especially during the first year of marriage to Micah.

I experienced so much deep loneliness. I went from so much time with friends to long days alone to nights waiting for him to get home from making his album after work with his best friend. I stuffed it all down with massive doses of pita chips and hummus mixed with Gilmore Girls on repeat for the next ten years.

The lingering loneliness never passed, a shadow I sought to outpace through rock climbing. It became a solace—I felt my lost power in climbing, my ability to turn gravity into dust. Watching the weight shift, I became one with the stone under my toes and my hands in complete harmony unifying me with the ancient rocks. Staring up at something so primordial, so strong, looking her in the eye, in the flickering minerals layered by wind and time, whispering to her, "You and I are the same." It became my reclamation, a place where gravity bowed to my will.

Rock climbing also became a dance between scaling heights, while battling occasional binge eating to stuff down further my fear of losing Micah's love. I'd mask it with more rocking, climbing, and running to make sure I wouldn't get fat. At least this was the bargaining I did in my head, trying to ensure I'd still be lovable when he was around.

Yet, amidst the cliffs, I rediscovered my body's language. In that embrace with the earth's rugged arms, I found new strength, embodying a true fierceness and power. Finally, I was at home with my incredible body.

As I began to heal, my protocol with food became one of my greatest allies in helping manage the symptoms of my illnesses. Food has had to morph from just nutrition, to fighting, to cure the alignments of all the hurts. And food can no longer be a comfort, nor a bargain, of my worth put into someone else's hands.

When I was sick, I could no longer stuff. I could only work short hours. I couldn't rock climb every evening. I couldn't go snowboarding. I couldn't binge all the comfort foods without more consequences of my body screaming back. Coping skills were no longer options. I had to become the one to sit in the dark hole with every single feeling.

Often, it felt exhausting, trying, and laborious, but it's also the most beautiful thing I've ever done for myself.

When I'm in the pit with them, asking them what they need, they often ask, "Can we just have a good hug or a big pile of tissues?"

Even on days when I was with Micah, I kept comforting them in the form of puppy cuddles alongside our Maltese, Toby. I encompassed myself with pillows and blankets while also surrounding myself with therapists and friends who understood my journey. I no longer needed to stuff myself so full. Providing myself with support, awareness of the inherited lies, and rewiring them led me to the most profound healing.

I once joined a women's group where we gathered to share something in our hearts. We came together to be vulnerable and have a space to be seen and heard without someone trying to fix us.

A woman shared that she feels so much but was terrified of sitting with any of her emotions because they might consume her. I remember experiencing the same things when I started to work with a therapist.

We all need a reminder to look into a future version of ourselves and see it's in the listening where we become free.

Seeing myself now, I witnessed someone with so much space to listen to every ounce of pain. Hindsight shows me that emotions don't drown us; they already engulf us. These very things we're trying to avoid, show us exactly how not to sink deeper into the numbness of ignorance.

In our numbness, we might as well be called death, for what is life if we are bonded to that which we fear and not free to choose how we exist?

No longer bonded to just coping, I've drank life to its brim. I'm drunk on every sensation, a tantalizing foundation that keeps me finding the roots of all that's gone numb so they can defrost and grow into the wind, dancing daily in unlocked freedom.

FIRST STAGE

Driving up to my first-ever open mic night, I parked near the street of the address listed. I saw the sign "Potter's House." Part of me felt betrayed that the flier did not say this was a church, but I knew before I even stepped foot inside that this was a church. Oh, how I wish it were some weird Harry Potter-themed gathering instead. I was so excited to finally share my writing.

I laughed at how absurd it was that my first time sharing my words would be with a similar group of people I left two years before declaring I was done with their sacrificial ways. Despite my judgments, I know these beautiful souls are hurt and are doing their best to find peace.

A few friendly faces welcomed me, and I inadvertently found myself at the table of the pastor's wife, Monica. She sat with her legs crossed and her body turned partly towards me as she waved to everyone who came in. She greeted a few people as they came to give her a hug and kiss on the cheek. She was in her realm, completely beloved. We sat waiting for the show to begin, and she asked me, "What do you believe about life after death?" These are the wild questions Christians ask strangers. To be fair, she did ask me one or two average questions before lining this one up.

Adjusting my legs as I sat in my chair, I leaned forward and replied with my simple truth, "I believe we all have our right to self-authorship. The power of god is within us all."

A question mark was plastered all over her face, as she then felt invited to share that she believed in being saved by a God and by Jesus. I find it ironic that she didn't want to hear my answer as much as she wanted me to hear her story. She now owed her entire life to him.

My heart sank deep into my belly at the thought of another person giving up their autonomy to find salvation outside their own two feet.

The repulsion rises within me because I remember doing the same. In high school, I often found myself ostracized because I felt pressure from my church to "spread the gospel." (A.k.a. go tell people about what you believe, even if they don't ask about it. So that they, too, can be saved from the destruction of hell—a made-up place we don't even know exists where all people who don't believe in what you think go after death.)

Texting with a friend in high school, she asked me outright, "Do you believe I'm going to hell?"

I replied, "Yes, because you don't believe in Jesus."

I wish I remembered what she said. Needless to say, my bible-thumping made me lose a lot of friends, get uninvited to places, and became very alone because no one else went to my church and believed all the same things I did.

I was placed third to be on stage that open mic night, but I was the only one not proclaiming my love for a savior.

Listening to person after person talk about being saved felt familiar and suffocating. I tried my best not to slip on my old sorting hat when I felt judged and unsafe. I remembered these are their stories and journeys. I don't need to invalidate or put them down to honor mine.

So I listened with caring eyes and heard the messages repeatedly. They were saved.

I thought I needed a savior, too. First, Jesus needed to cleanse my heart of all the ugly things I would do when no one was looking. Things like touching myself, even though my family normalized masturbation; along with horrific nicknames that normalized and justified the sexual abuse. But now I look back and realize that my family, full of shoved-under-the-rug trauma, taught me to lie more than to tell the truth.

After getting sick in my twenties, going to therapy, learning about trauma, boundaries, and even abuse, I realized it wasn't anything outside of me that healed me. My behaviors weren't the problem. It was the deep grief inside of me that I'd been carrying for years. I realized I had to become my savior. No one else was going to rescue me. The power of that realization brought me precisely to where I am today.

Sitting in easily stackable metal chairs with soft cushions at this church open mic, I heard the derailing of the railroad track they had all been stuck on. "I was molested my whole life…I got into drugs, and then Jesus saved my life." Story after story: "I was suicidal and attempted to kill myself until I found hope in Jesus." The patterns matched up in each story. Everyone saw their life turning around due to Jesus.

It took all of me not to want to go back up on stage after I shared my piece and say, "Don't you see it was you who brought you to stop? You had faith in you!"

My heart broke into all the wooden pieces now nailed up on the back wall, just like the story of their savior; the one they believed had to sacrifice for their whole. Except, I'm not sacrificing. I'm holding space, honoring myself and their journey.

I'm glad they found their out, their hope, their happiness, but my heart breaks the most because I hope they never forget it was them in the end—this beautiful spark in their hearts that rescued them, that helped them see there could be another way to live. Everyone in the room, including myself, had this in common.

While sitting in my chair as I listened to their stories, I wished these people had more support and more loving voices to tell them their pain was real. More support to help them see what happened to them wasn't a sin. It is the repetition of trauma, unspoken feelings, and misplaced anger that leads to so much suffering afflicted upon ourselves and others, tangled in a web of environments, genetics, and lack of privileges to heal. My heart breaks knowing too many humans are stuck in this horrible cycle.

Finally, the open mic night ended with an altar call, a peculiar tradition at the end of church experiences or services where they ask anyone who feels called to ask Jesus into their heart and be saved. When we witness how someone else is healing and say, "I want that too," something in us finally snaps, and we see we can have a different life. I love this ability we have in us. I hope more will see they can do it by following the truth within themselves, too.

Even though I had so many more words to share than just the ones I'd spoken up on stage, I left the open mic night when the altar call began.

I hope all the people I stood before that night believe they'll find their internal power, whether they call it Jesus Christ or Spirit. And I hope they don't get too lost trying to make others believe all they do, but remember the great message of everything is always love. It's the most incredible message he ever taught, the one they all so beautifully adore within Jesus. I hope, if anything, they remember this message the most—it's the one I'll never forget.

The story of Jesus is one piece that I had all wrong. Except now, I know love doesn't mean sacrifice. Great loves do not sacrifice; they stand bravely in audacity to name themselves worthy of being one with God, being powerful, and turning microscopic, faith mustard seeds into mountains that move previously known realities.

Love is more powerful than we know, but our brains want someone else to fix us so we don't have to take responsibility for undoing all the mess. Untangling is the hardest part: the sweeping up of the patterns passed down.

I'm weary of it, to a fault. I'm tired of patterns, the messages repeatedly duplicating in my head. But each day, I'll shout back and remind myself that I'm my greatest savior and remember the love we all have. This strength grows more substantial the louder we get, shattering those chains of what kept us small. It's not sin. It's not satan. It's pain perpetuating itself.

Let's not blanket pain anymore with the blood of someone else. Instead, let's build an awareness of it. To name it as deep fear, then let love lather this pain and our heart's brokenness with all the tenderness our skin knows how to touch.

I know you believe in miracles. I do, too. This hard work we all must do is possible.

Let's take responsibility for the pain that's been done to us and the pain we've caused; remembering love is our greatest weapon. Use it tenderly and fiercely in your heart, but please don't wave it at anyone to cut off their truth of what's made them feel whole.

We all deserve to be seen.

We all deserve the freedom to be pure magic that shifts the matrix of reality, selling us the lie that we only deserve to be worthless worms about to die.

HE BROKE THE ~~MATRIX~~

I've made a promise to myself to unlearn a lie I grew up being told
was the truth: you must die to yourself to know how to be alive,
following the steps of Christ.

As I unraveled the layers of this inside of me,
I wanted to scream from the rooftops and shout,
"I saw a ghost, and it was myself!
        The one you told me to make there with your ancient lies.
           The one there with your pepper spray dosing my eyes.
               You cannot, and you will not steal my I."

I was gifted to be in this generation where we get to reclaim the self,
and see the value of what Jesus really was here to say.
As he himself audaciously proclaimed it, *God and I are one.*

Yes, follow his steps because it was he who bent the matrix,

this reality we all create inside of ourselves.
He showed us how to heal time.
But most of all, he showed us what it meant to love thy self.
Not as worthless worms needing to be sacrificed.
Not as abandoning every ounce of knowing,
rather digging into giving from the overflowing.

He calls us to have faith as big as a mustard seed;
that really was the message to say—
have faith in the impossible, and you'll quickly see
you hold the magic to shake every ounce of reality.

ENDING ATONEMENT

I spit out blood in the sink. My nose dripped with the same earlier that day, and I wondered if it was not a war going on inside, but a relearning of how to stop the sacrifice. It's all I've ever known most of my life. It's written in "Christ's blood" that we drank every Sunday morning in church as we took communion. Sacrifice. It's in the chains tied to my mother's feet. It's keeping her with the man who's abused her, me, and who knows how many others. He comes back apologizing a thousand times, promising he'll be better. Sacrifice. It had me anchored just the same to a man who never truly desired me but how good I could make him feel. I believed I had to sacrifice to sustain my daughter's safety with the anchor knotted around my throat and chest, keeping me from saying "No."

Until a cough parted from my lips, exhaling out the truth my lungs already knew. "We cannot continue on this way."

One summer during the pandemic when I was still married to Micah, one of my many therapists asked me, "Don't you deserve to be happy, too?" She seemingly disappeared as the stars do at noon.

I guess she sacrificed too much trying to help so many. And the burnt-out, like all of us who are asked to give more than we have finally pushed her to call it quits.

However, my life is, thankfully, very different now. I'm no longer bound to the death of self, as religion tells us to do. I'm actively ending the generational trauma inherited from my family. I now surround myself with people who know my value. Now, sacrifice isn't inked on my skin covered in rashes; it's not in my daily habits, and it is not the story to which I find my basic needs met.

I've been parting ways with her. Sacrifice, the one that drives nails into wrists. She'll set it on a cross and declare, "This is the only way."

To proclaim such things is to believe only in gray while ignoring every rainbow after a storm, every sunrise on a less cloud-covered day, and the sunset that reflects on the ocean's waves.

Me? I see color.

I saw this magic recently as the sun descended the hills of my valley, crossed with rivers parting its path. The reminder set in. If such beauty exists everyday, how can life be created only for sacrifice and suffering to exist? It has to be beautiful, just like this.

Yet, symptoms flared in me. The blood spilled out of me. A cough lingered in my lungs. The blood purged from my teeth just being touched with a floss. The weight in my chest ached with its involuntary explosions. The fire in my root groaned. The ache on my tongue pulsed. The swelling in my toes and my hands doubled their size. The pain is numb when it grows too loud to stand upright. I am ready to break up with the suffering inside of me.

"No more sacrifice, please. Can we all just get along?" I wanted to shout to all the loud exclamations inside of me.

Doctors once told me that my body was attacking itself. I heard this glorious queen of a woman I've come to adore say the same today of this beautiful butterfly organ in her throat. I wanted to shout, "No, no! It's beautiful. It's not hurting itself. There is something else!" But instead, all that came out of my lungs was this cough that wanted to show me something of my heart. This reminder, "You also need to remember—this is something else."

The pain I've been living with most of my life; a new intersection must be built for this to budge.

My heart was heavy and exasperated. Maybe I was just a terrible listener because all I wanted to do was proclaim my worth with how magical I could be and take care of myself all alone. "Thank you very much!" As I crossed my arms and puffed my bottom lip.

Then, a whisper came in as I went to sit in meditation with all my symptoms flaring. "This will not move forward until you believe with every cell, you are perfect. You are enough just for being."

In my refusal, I crawled. I scraped and groveled at anything nearby, finding more bleeding, and shouted, "Let me show you how wonderful I am!" As if proving my worth was the only way out of the suffering I existed in.

A gentle hand rested on my shoulder, lifting my ground-turned, groveling chin.

"My dear, you do not need to prove yourself.
If you must dig, dig in the dirt and plant your seeds.
If you must be on your hands and knees,
kiss the flowers good morning.
If you must scrape,
scrape off the mud from your eyelids
that block out the beauty in all you see.
If you must grovel,
let yourself discover the bee taking a nap
inside the blooming of a flower.
If you must bleed,
let it be the blood of the berries you picked,
turning your tongue purple.
But, never, my dear,
let it be to prove your worth for that is as simple as—I am."

"I am." Is this the new crossroad? Or is it also uncovering the truth buried along with the body of Christ? He declared it when he said, "God and I are One."

When John wrote, "In the beginning was the Word, and the Word was with God, and the Word was God."[1] , maybe this was the real message he meant for us to receive when he told us to follow in his footsteps. Remember, we are all one. We all are creators.

What will I believe? Sacrifice: a war. Or a mystery I've never understood. I think it's in this whisper I hear so faintly, this marvelous internal wisdom I've come to trust more than any sacrificial blood.

---

1. 1 John 1:1 KJV

WAY OF THE TRIBE

In an age of independence, where mothers often feel pressured to navigate everything independently, we had to learn the ways of the tribe. How many mothers bear the weight of a system built over generations, where time and energy are shared and support is readily available? This existence is unfamiliar to most modern mothers. Still, my daughter Olea and I experienced it for our own survival. While it would have been ideal to have a choice in the matter, I embraced the journey we embarked on as the right one for us.

During the early years of Olea's childhood, there were days when I had to beg for help. Most days, caring for myself, let alone my daughter, was more than I could physically do. I was barely able to get out of the bed I shared with Micah that was placed on the floor because we wanted a king size from the amount of times I'd disrupt him in his sleep. I reached out to friends, flooding their phones with requests for assistance, as I knew my Doodle Ma'am, Olea's nickname, needed more than I could provide.

"Hi everyone. Is anyone available to help me with Olea today? I'm having a high symptom day and unable to do much."

Many turned me down or didn't respond, perhaps feeling just as helpless themselves.

"I'm so sorry you are. Praying for you," a mother of two would reply.

"I have my own appointments today, sorry." Micah's mom would respond as she, too, battled health issues.

The exhaustion that plagues most mothers is all too familiar in their sleepless eyes. But a few said yes.

"Of course. She's more than welcome here. Daniel can be over in an hour to pick her up." Jennifer would often reply. She was a stay-at-home mom with long brown hair and determination to make life beautiful, which she so often did by holding stunning space for everyone to fill up their 700-square-foot home with shaggy old carpets and no dishwasher. She had three kids under five but was one of those women who had the capacity for so much.

Often, mothers like Jennifer would provide like the mother and the caretaker I could not be that day.

Sometimes, I wonder how I could detach from Olea so quickly. I let her go off with other mothers with no jealousy. And even now, as I co-parent half of the time, my heart breaks every time we have to say goodbye. I miss the house filled with her footsteps and giggles that echo on every wall, but it's easy to get lost in worlds without her. And now I understand why. We'd been practicing being apart starting at age three, even though we desperately wanted to hold each other close.

We formed a deep bond for the first two years, fortunate enough to breastfeed whenever we desired. Of all the motherly tasks of raising a child, baking together and nursing were my two absolute favorites. We'd often sit cuddling on the couch, smiling at each other. It is one of the most beautiful things I've had the privilege of doing with her.

However, the development of the rashes and the horrific pain the rashes were causing forced us to stop nursing before we were ready.

"You'll need to stop nursing if you are to get these rashes to clear up," my doctor told me as I was sitting on the crunchy patient paper.

"Ok. My daughter is two. I think we'll be ok."

I went home and grieved we had to stop. The next time Olea asked, "Can I have mommy's milk?" I had to tell her we could not. So we swapped out our ancient connection with cuddles and longer bedtime snuggles.

Sadly though, for the following two years, Olea often asked, "Can I have mommy's milk?" and even asked, "If one day I get another sister, can I have mommy's milk then?"

Full of grief but trying to hold it together, I always replied, "I'm sorry, my dear. There is none left to give."

Then, as if that wasn't enough to give up on her, my joints swelled and doubled their size. More doctor instructions came.

"You need to stop picking up your daughter. She's old enough to walk now. You could be continually hurting yourself," my doctor proclaimed.

Covered in joint supports, I had to stop holding my daughter conventionally. We had to learn how to let me slip my forearms under her armpits and have her grip on me so I could pick her up. We got creative in how I could hold her without my wrists, but it shattered us both, nonetheless.

At age two, she transitioned from the crib's rails to a twin pillow-top mattress while many children her size still occupied barred beds. Guard rails were a savior for the days when I needed her to get out of bed, get dressed, and come to see if mommy could be her mommy that day. Someone else would usually whisk her away if I couldn't. She would find solace in the home of a close friend, surrounded by new toys and temporary siblings she longed for just as much as "mommy's milk."

These temporary families met her needs while I laid in bed, tears streaming down my face, trying to find a sense of aliveness amidst the turmoil that had turned my world upside down, as doctors told me my body was "attacking itself."

Labeling our experience as "tragic" is easy, with her childhood and our bond snatched away from us. But that's only one side of the story I can choose to hold onto. There are always more sides than what meets the eye: the front and back, the left and right, and the edges and corners in between. Two can always be divided into two. Let me describe it differently: this top corner, and that bottom piece in the southwest. I am now doing my best to rewrite our narrative, transforming it from a tragedy into a beautiful tale of self-discovery.

Olea grew up within a tribe of many mothers, fathers, and siblings that changed with the tide. Many loved and cherished her while I had the space to confront the demons lurking in my closet of grief called suppressed trauma.

Others in my lineage did not ever have the space to heal. So, I had to figure out how to move out of just existing to an embodiment of being without the need to numb out. It was a gift from the lens I can see through today. These salt-stained cheeks forever hold this pain of the grief of being a disability unseen. This pain has felt greater than words could ever fit in any book or library, for that fact. Yet, I choose compassion daily, for both Olea and myself, to see the lessons buried in the graves of all we lost.

I wouldn't wish this journey upon anyone, but it is uniquely mine. I am grateful for the spaces it led me to, allowing me to heal wounds that had never been healed before me. I have unearthed generational scars through this journey, given them names, and banished them from the shadows. I've recognized their fallacies and declared they will never be part of my new inner galaxy or Olea's heart. They end here, at these shoes, sitting by the door, belonging thankfully to *no body*.

IF IT'S ANCIENT IT MUST BE TRUE

Echoes in my mind insist, "They must come first. I must ensure they have enough before I can care for myself." A historic decree etched in aged papyrus reverberates a narrative disempowering women, its ink seeping into the fabric of our existence."

I'm weary of this cycle. From the moment we draw our first breath, we, as women, are taught about sacrificial love. We internalize the idea that being born implies separation from our mothers. But is this true, or have we painted our reality in shades of gray?

"Love requires sacrifice."

Do you genuinely believe that?

I used to. Raised with religious teachings, I learned about a savior who sacrificed his life for my salvation. My mother, too, constantly sacrificed her own needs to ensure our survival. She loved us with all she had left after working a full-time job and caring for my sister and I, often alone, while my dad traveled for work. We frequently found her asleep on the couch or cuddling us in bed, exhausted from trying to do it all. She repeatedly denied her needs for the sake of us. I see this pattern in many parents and even in myself with my daughter. It took me years to realize I deserved to be happy and to leave her dad, who wasn't interested in the deep relationship I desired. I had it ingrained in my head that I had to sacrifice my well-being so a divorce wouldn't damage her. Yet, it was denying my basic need to be cherished by my partner that was doing us all so much harm. Religion, my mother's example, and culture taught me that motherhood meant giving up parts of myself.

When I gave birth to my daughter, I almost entirely sacrificed myself. I felt my soul depart my body as if I was drifting away from life. Honesty, it was the most peaceful I'd ever felt, free from the excruciating pain that had plagued me for over twenty-four hours. The attachment to my physical self dissolved, and everything felt beautifully iridescent.

Then, his voice pulled me back. Micah said, "I think we need help."

I couldn't be present then because I had given too much and needed support. After receiving medical assistance, my daughter was born twelve hours later. And in those hours, I felt the weight of my sacrifices pulling me away from the very essence of motherhood.

Two years after my daughter was born, my body continued to scream through a manifestation of chronic illnesses. I became a mother working from home, photographing long wedding events during summer and fall weekends, managing a household, and caring for a daughter who refused to sleep through the night with constant cries no one, including myself, could explain or soothe; although solace was frequently found in "mommy's milk." To bring her into this world, I had given so much of myself to be her source.

For years afterward, amidst the pain, rashes, debilitating fatigue, and disabilities, my body screamed, "We need support! I'm not ok. We're not okay. We need this bed. We need more care. Will you come to love us?"

"You cannot do as you please." Its cries were louder than the needs of my child or my ex-husband.

I had to close my successful wedding photography business of seven years because the excruciating pain made it impossible for me to hold a camera, let alone button my pants. My body screamed louder asking, "Will you please take care of me? You can no longer sacrifice."

In this bed named Rest, the four-letter word I wish never existed, I faced the realities of all I was told by ancient ink that I had to sacrifice. I was once an active person, dancing, bike riding, and rock climbing weekly, snowboarding every winter, and constantly in motion. Yet, my body declared daily, "Right here, in this place, you'll find the lie that too many have dressed in moss. We're here for you to discover you are not the green fuzz. You are more like the brown of a branch—a dormant seed waiting to burst into vibrant life. No more sprawling out on the ground and collecting mildew with every storm."

After years of neglecting my body's needs, it finally became a symphony I could no longer ignore. The bed of Rest beckoned me each day, allowing my body to declare the truths I needed to hear and understand why I felt this deep, ceaseless suffering.

In my struggle for survival and to become a witness of myself, I discovered that this suffering stemmed from the lie that I had to give up myself to create. In reality, creativity is innate.

So now, I proclaim:

"Farewell, sacrifice. I am ready to sever all ties, and I am grateful that circumstances have forced us apart. No more of it; it's time to love this seed of myself where we are truly a root, one that multiplies each year. We won't break beneath the ground, for we have no volatility. When we burst out of our shell, the sprout will emerge, piercing the tender soil to touch the sun for the first time."

We do not need more generations of sacrifice. Instead, let us become a generation that knows how to love ourselves, honor our emotions, delve deep into our desires, and chase what illuminates our souls.

RE-MOTHERING

Just two days had passed since I'd last seen Olea. She spends part of her time with me in our snug 300-square-foot studio apartment nestled near the foothills of Mt. Tabor, a dormant volcano. In the forest full of towering trees, we often rambled around after school, exploring the playground. Our apartment had room for my bed, a hutch for my office, and an alcove perfectly fitted with a bunk bed for her, complete with draping curtains to create a room-like feel. A golden light fixed on the wall offered her a warm reading nook before bedtime.

Often, I'd pick her up at her Waldorf school twenty minutes from where we lived. Gathering with her classmates under a tent that protected them from the rain, they waited for pick up. Once she saw me, she would often run through the mushy grass, splattering mud on her rainboots with her arms spread wide like she was about to take flight. This feeling is the gift of motherhood I've been able to give to her: freedom to be entirely her. I weep at this proud moment and acknowledge my inner child, wishing I had that same safety growing up. Yet, I gently remind my inner child I've been re-mothering her, too.

One day, as seven-year-old Olea and I drove home from school, she told me she was frustrated. From her booster seat in the back, she explained, "Kevin, a student in my class, was frustrated today. I tried to help him feel better. Except he wouldn't. And he just stayed grumpy." I felt the exasperation in her.

This familiar story was one I'd known all too well: a person feeling responsible for making the sad person happy. Oh, how many years I had tried to do the same thing to her dad, Micah, who faced deep depression and lack of self-worth daily. I, too, once believed if I loved him enough, he would be happy.

Each day, he'd come home from his job at the lighting company and drop his bags full of books he'd read between serving customers, along with his body. He'd sit on the couch, and I'd bound over to him. I'd sit next to him, on his lap, or cuddle him as I scratched his arms. He absolutely adored this one place of touch, which sent him into a trance. He'd gush about all his big feelings. It felt like I'd puff him up after work like a deflated balloon. Still, he couldn't sustain the inflation, so he relied on my helium. Yet, he never came to appreciate me more than for how I could make him feel, so I, too, soon became empty.

I witnessed too many women, like my mother, being the rescuers to everyone in their lives, too.

My mom, to this day, does the same to my dad. Whenever he is upset, she feels responsible for making him feel better. As a child, he'd come home angry about something that happened at work. My mom would walk around the kitchen with him, often "talking him down." Telling him it was okay and that everything would be better soon. And I thought that was my job as a wife until it cost me every-thing I had, including my happiness and health.

That was when I said no to the end of this repeated storyline. But here, Olea was doing the same, just like she'd been taught by watch-ing me for seven years with Micah.

My heart wrenched and curled like the puckering of lips after they had sucked on a lemon too long. Shame wanted to fill my mouth. I showed Olea this pattern with seven years of sacrificial love.

Generations have passed this down before. This is how we eng-age with people: we control them so that we feel better, we regulate them so we feel okay too, and we sacrifice ourselves in hopes that we'll find the peace we long for that's right here pulsing in the veins of our own skin.

I took a deep breath in my regulation. I paused to listen to Olea, trying my best to explain how to not replicate the history that took me thirty-three years to overcome. Yet, here is the absolute most incredible gift.

In the best way I could share, I said, "You cannot make your friends feel better. No matter how much you want to. You have to let people feel their feelings."

Frustration boiled to the top of her inner volcano about to erupt. The molten lava ran down the side of her. It made her end her story; exploding with, "But if I don't help him, everyone else will be frus-trated because we always have to stop the lesson when he's frustrated. So then, I'll be frustrated too because we cannot learn anything." She crossed her arms and snuffed.

I let her fume. Paused. Then noted, "That sounds overwhelming."

I'm thankful for my counselors at this moment. They taught me this flip: acknowledge instead of fix. Give the awareness the other lacks.

And so, it was with that same formula that I reminded her, "Olea, you have a beautiful heart that wants to help people, and your whole class. But sometimes, we need to feel all of our emotions. How would you feel if every time you were sad, I tried to make you feel better right away?"

"Not very good." Suddenly, her eyes brightened, and a proverbial light bulb clicked on in her head.

"Maybe I should ask him if he wants help calming down next time. It wouldn't feel good if I was frustrated or sad and someone tried to make me feel better unless they asked. I'll try that next time."

My heart grew the size of Alaska with this amazing little girl I call "daughter." Her pure love for people, and helping them to feel good is her greatest gift; as well as her awareness to see, compare, and find solutions so quickly when all she needs from me is just to help her see she has it all along—right there in her.

I cannot believe I get to be her witness in this life.

She descended from her loft bed later that evening, dressed up in a crop top swimsuit, with a clock over her head, hat on her head, and headphones covering her ears. She spread her arms out wide, speaking as if she was on stage using my name. She's watching my every move, my every breath, and thoughts across my face. I feel joy knowing this because Shame and I have broken up, and I'm stepping into new layers of my skin, which I can only hope she'll find, too.

I wanted to imprint this newfound wisdom into our daily lives. It was a truth I yearned to share, especially with Olea, my beacon of boundless love and empathy.

It took me thirty-three years to shatter the truths she fought with today, and because of this crushing I've been doing, it took her thirty minutes for it to click, with me simply holding space for her to see.

I wanted to hug my past self when I questioned if I deserved to be happy after I left her dad and tell her it's okay. This is what she'll know: that we don't have to sacrifice ourselves to make others happy. We get to hold space for them and find all we need right here in our very own bones.

FINDING YOUR PLACE

Navigating the landscape of chronic illnesses was like searching for my seat in the classroom with my eyes blinded and my hearing gone. No one was directing me, and I felt like I lost my ability to choose my reality. We can easily find our place in society in a world that values our abilities to match others. But your place seems nonexistent and invisible if you don't have the same capabilities. The people who contribute the greatest are valued the most. However, we are wired for connection, to be part of a community, to play a role in something larger than ourselves. So, I found myself lost, often unknowing where I belonged.

Paradoxically, our world feels more isolated than ever. Post-pandemic, we're all hungry for human connection, trying to search for it on a black mirror we hold in our pockets. Only to find that other's lives are seemingly more beautiful than ours, while getting reminders of all the things we could be. We saturate ourselves more with envy than with our blood. We question why we endure such profound depression and anxiety when, as a culture, we haven't allowed ourselves space to be lost, unfound, and in the process of becoming.

Over a decade ago, I carved out my niche as a mountain wedding photographer. Beloved clients cherished my art, and even now, I receive inquiries from brides who desire my unique touch.

A bride set up a phone call with me after hearing I had photographed at the same wedding venue she was getting married at, the University of Denver. "I saw your photos, and they were stunning. We're getting married in the same place as your photos, and I wanted to know if you're available?"

Covering the grief with an icing of polite responses, I replied, "Oh my goodness. Thank you. I wish I were available, but I no longer photograph larger weddings in Denver. Here are some other photographers I know." While steering her toward others, I secretly wished that I could still be the one capturing their most treasured moments.

I found my niche in an industry that celebrated love and stories. Being a visual storyteller has been one of my greatest joys. My craft allowed me to immerse myself in the richness of life, capturing its essence right at its heart. It was a fusion of all the elements I held dear: the spark of a new chapter, the accumulation of community coming together, the details of decor that reflected the beauty of the couple's love, and breathtaking locations holding them into the firmness of the Colorado Rocky Mountains all sandwiched into one incredible day. I was able to help my couples remember each stunning moment, the ones they saw, and the ones that happened because they chose to celebrate in this unique way. I ate it up like a little kid stepping into a candy store for the first time after being told they could try every last treat.

Then, my body became louder than my ability. Just six years into a thriving business, my rashes grew worse, even with doctor-prescribed steroids, along with joint pain that quickly developed. Doctors thought it was from overuse, so I had to stop picking up anything over a few pounds, including my camera with its lenses. Within a year, I lost mobility in both my wrists, resulting in two wrist braces.

I could not do basic tasks like scrubbing dishes, holding a phone to text, or lifting groceries into my car without inflicting horrific pain.

Meanwhile, my business finally had couples lining up to book with me two years in advance. My schedule was at capacity, and I was hiring other people to support me to continue to do the things I love. I was pulling in income for my family, but suddenly I had to stop.

A chasm opened within when I had to close my business. The creation I'd painstakingly built across two states, a manifestation of my soul, had vanished in the blink of an eye. Grief filled me, but I didn't have space to weep. I quickly replaced every ounce of my energy with doctor appointments and symptoms that grew louder inside me, unable to express any of my grief.

Nearly a decade has elapsed since that turning point, and I've healed a lot. I'm no longer bed-bound. I can now grasp a camera again, but it took another few years before I built back the endurance to stand for hours. Even though I tried to regrow my business, I've realized that I can't be the artist I once was—disabilities have reshaped the canvas I create with.

During my journey, I embraced the role of a yoga teacher, envisioning a community where I could impart the healing wisdom I found through this beautiful practice. Yet, that path, too, was curtailed when the church changed its mind about allowing yoga classes.

After a year of creating classes at my local church, I gathered mothers and people with flexible schedules to enjoy caring for themselves and diving into their hearts on their yoga mats. Near the end of the classes, our pastor even joined and said, "That was incredibly healing. It felt good to get out of the mind and into my body. It felt like I was interweaving scripture into my body."

He returned after a church meeting later to tell me, "Not everyone is okay with yoga practices, despite you bringing it into Christianity. So we have to stop having classes here."

After that, I was done with letting men tell me how I would live my life.

Undeterred, I dove into other trainings and other curiosities for healing, hoping to fuse my healing journey with my passion for helping others. (Ironically, in this endeavor, I learned that the most profound healing often arises from those who have navigated their own odysseys of recovery.)

In hindsight, I revisited a video series I once created on self-love. The beauty and potency of those lessons struck me—gems hidden away in the shadows of a webpage, accumulating zero views over the years. Defeatism loomed like a shadow compared to the peak I experienced as a photographer.

A feeling of disconnection settled in. It's easy to feel adrift in a world designed for the able-bodied. However, we mustn't perpetuate this cycle of ableism. Our worth isn't weighted on our actions. We are worthy of everything because we exist.

Despite limitations, we possess incredible capacities. Grieve all the sorrows you need, maybe even more than you thought. Yet, resist the urge to cast ourselves as victims. I, for one, refuse to let my life become a tragedy. Instead, I strive for a life that is the most salacious romantic comedy that inspires others to remember, they, too, can have the existence that romances them every damn day; knowing I am worthy of being right here, right now. Discovering each day, it's not anyone else's story—I am meant to tell it all. My place in the classroom of life is still as the beloved storyteller. This time, not of other journeys but my own, my beautiful, mundane, magical, blooming life.

BRIGHT LIGHTS

Walking inside the medical building, I looked at the unit number on my calendar: 300, level three. I was on ground three. Torn between the elevator with no ventilation in the middle of the most contagious strain of the pandemic, I decided the stairwell looked more pleasing. This day was a rare day for me, as I wasn't rushing. I'd arrived with plenty of time to get to my appointment. (Something I historically never did, trying to squeeze too much in a day to prove "I'm enough.")

Bounding up the stairs, I felt excited to do this. I hadn't wanted to take the stairs up before, but I wanted to now because I could. "Look, I'm healing. I can do this!" I wanted to shout to anyone passing by, even though I was the only one in the stairwell.

Puffing, I reached the top. My face was covered in my special mask, the same brand I had before masks were normal because my doctors recommended them to protect me while traveling. My body knew unwanted pathogens were home like my abuser made himself cozy inside me despite my pleas shouting, "No!" It's confusing, and

I'm trying my best to show her what is okay. It began with declaring my no's as a one hundred percent no. Now I'm older. Now I'm stronger. Now, I'm building safety.

I opened the door and felt the memories instantly. The fluorescent lights hit my skin, and my body reacted, flooding me with dizziness and feelings of powerlessness. I'm afraid I was wrong. Maybe I hadn't healed as much as I thought.

The receptionist had this empty look. She didn't interact. She simply directed. "Give me your information," short and to the point.

"Where has the human gone?" I wanted to ask, but I signed the paperwork she required without saying a word.

She asked, "Is this still your address?" pointing to the Milwaukie one. I shook my head and gave her the new Portland one where I was pouring out my truths as the rain soaked my winter window pane.

Despite wishing I was fully healed, the room began to spin. I was torn between the urge to use the restroom and the need to sit before my body made me feel like it had so many times before. I used to get so dizzy from low blood pressure that I passed out. The doctors have called this P.O.T.S. But this, I know, is a trauma response. I hadn't felt this in two years. This much turmoil made the room spin like I'd been star-tripping or on the merry-go-round at high speed with my eyes closed and then trying to be still.

I reached the bathroom seat and found the nurse had called, but I was gone.

I stepped out of the restroom to find her impatiently waiting for me. No greeting, just opening a door directing me where to go as if I were an airplane about to land and not a human needing care.

Taking off my jacket, I set my purse down where she instructed me. I stood on the scale and noticed my body had exploded a sixteenth of its size. I tried to hold it together to make it to my room, still feeling this sense of spinning. Once I arrived in the room, I sat on a paper-covered bed and tried my best to distract myself.

I noticed the instruments needed for today's check-up appointment, the only annual one I do. I forgot my preferred lubricant, coconut oil. My breath shortened even more, and I tried to tell my body it would be ok.

My doctor came in and greeted me. She is kind and willing to listen. She asked me if I had my oil today, telling me how she's also shared that with her other sensitive patients. She proclaims she learned that from me!

I thought internally, "What did my ears hear? A physician who appreciates learning from a patient and thanking them?" I wanted to hug her, but I smiled behind my mask instead.

She asked to draw blood for the sixteenth-size expansion. I agreed and mentioned I was feeling extra lightheaded. She calmed my concerns and asked if I needed water or a snack. Sadly, many people always think my dizziness is my blood sugar. But it's not. It's the P.O.T.S. I wanted to reply, "No. Water and snacks won't do, just the trauma of my soul ripped apart in my childhood. My body is just trying its best to be whole." But again, I stayed quiet.

After our check-up, I took the elevator down this time, to the labs on level 1. There was no interaction, and no greeting from this receptionist either. I was just given paperwork and directions. I had no wit and no joy to offer because I was just doing my best to stand upright. Maybe we all are; but I wished it were another way, where when we saw each other, we only lit up in escalating joy.

"Will you please use the butterfly needle? You'll struggle to find my veins without it." I shared with the nurse as she prepared to draw my blood, opening the sanitary packages and placing a sticker with my name on the vials. "I tend to pass out, too. Can you make sure only to take as little as you need?" The nurse nodded and instructed me to lie down.

As she shuffled off to gather more supplies, I pulled my knees into my chest, hoping to help the blood flow stay in my head and heart to remain conscious.

She returned with the standard-size needle and more supplies. I saw it in her eyes. She was determined to do things her way.

The needle plunged into my skin, and she struggled to get it to flow. I had warned her. My body refused to give away its precious blood. But she pulled on my skin until she removed the needle and went to ask for help.

Another nurse came in. They got it to flow. They took a vial full of blood, still not listening to my requests, and my body was angry.

Why am I just another machine in this world? Is this what Western medicine has done? Viewing us so much as bits and pieces that we are no longer whole humans?

My eyes were closed, trying to stay whole. With the sound of a loud snap, I knew they'd finish their work as they removed their gloves. My body knows that sound all too well. Sometimes, it feels as if because I've been through so much, I'm unsafe to touch.

Yet, as I rage in my hurt, the trauma I see continues around me, and I'm also a perpetrator disregarding even my flesh and blood's requests.

In our apartment the next day, Olea requested clothes other than the ones I gave her.

"Everything didn't feel right, mommy. My arms, my legs, it's tight everywhere."

"You're just fussing. Once you get to play, you'll feel fine." I replied to her in our apartment, trying to leave quickly for a playdate we were already late for.

But here, I am doing the same. Teaching Olea to ignore the screaming messages of her body's discomfort.

Is this the message from our bodies we all grow up learning to ignore? Is it just something you need to push past?

I want to cringe. I want to shout. "No! Please, this cannot be our truth!"

Back in the lab offices, finally, they are done. I found my breath again and struggled to stand up, so I took it slow. I began by sitting up cross-legged because it helps the blood pool in my legs and stays more in my brain. Ten minutes went by, and then I tried to walk. I bargain with myself, wishing to escape this vacuum of disconnect. "If I can make it outside, maybe this will pass."

Stepping slowly out the door without a single soul noticing, I made it to my car and sat there, still waiting to trust myself enough to drive.

Internally, I questioned, "Who would I call today? My new boyfriend, Moon? I'm not ready for him to see me this sick. We've only known each other for six months. My ex-husband? Oh, I cannot need him again. A car service? Oh, but it's dangerous to be with so many new people during the pandemic." I sighed and hoped this would pass.

I tried my best to do some mind-numbing tasks for twenty more minutes.

Finally, relief came and I drove home. Immediately, I crawled into bed. That day, I wished I had a mobility aid and that handicap sign that expired in October when I'd hoped to be healed by now. It broke the day I delivered Moon his birthday package, one of the wild things that started our connection. But it's still expired and broken.

I wanted it to be a metaphor, to be healed with this new chapter. With this new chapter, I hoped to be better by now.

Yet, as I dove into my subconscious later that afternoon in my meditation practice, my body showed me she remembered the times I'd been sick in my life when I didn't know. I got ill when I was three months old. I had to be hospitalized and placed inside an oxygen tent because I struggled to breathe. I'd seen too much in my mother's womb. I think I knew how my dad stole from her, too. My soul wanted to leave too soon. This is too much. But they pulled me back, and I fought for the letter my grandmother Julia wrote to me.

"Hang on, my little angel," she told me as she glared through the tent. Her smile, she saw me. She'd always seen me and loved me with all she had.

She'd known hospitals too much, too, with the loss of two children. One in a toilet before it attached, and another who took his life too early in his twenties. She'd fought with another granddaughter for too many days in these fluorescent-filled rooms. I wanted to stay with her too. My body recalled this sensation. It's been battling for life since an early age. Through this experience, I was reminded not to surrender. Rather than fighting, I'm learning to listen even more deeply to her. You'd think after learning to listen, that would be enough, but this level of listening goes deeper. I'm no longer striving just to survive. There's no need to search for more battles. We're in the process of embracing ease, moving gently, and letting go of the urge to push. We're rekindling the understanding that reality is shaped by us and the meanings we give it.

Right here beside you, I'm re-teaching myself that I matter and you matter. Together, let's break the cycle of repeatedly forgetting our own worth and the worth of one another. I'm discovering that our bodies hold immense wisdom, a voice that needs to be heard. So, let's reclaim friendship with our bodies. Even as our culture exclaims, we should ignore them.

SPARK THE FIRES OF LIGHT

She is not quiet.
She is loud and fierce.
She is bold and passionate.
In everything that she steps into,
she doesn't just dip her toes in.
She dives straight into the deep end,
ready to fully drink in every ounce of life.
She knows the preciousness of time and of life,
that nothing is more urgent
then needing to devour and be devoured.
It isn't sacrificial but a given offering
of the overflow in which she exists.
Dance with me, darling.
We're touching the stars
to spark the fires of the light
we all forgot we had.
Reignite the embers that are faint.

We're calling it depression and anxiety
because our souls ache for more than watching.
They desire embodying full fledged inhalation of the flame that
ignites our souls.

My beloved, you are not depressed.
You are lost watching,
witnessing too much
instead of living in the fire of your passions.
Reignite them.
Let them burn the depths of you.
Hunger you from the inside out.
Let them turn out all the filth you've collected,
telling you to play small,
that you are not enough.
You are enough for being here.
Please don't ever forget.

With every breath is your entire being shouting
LIVE LIVE LIVE!

Dance, sing, BE LOUD!

Be heard!

Be I AM!
Don't play small anymore.
You are not hidden in the molehill.
You are the top of the chain,
and that which you create trickles down.
Don't spread your fear.
Spread your abundant love
in the power of your fingertips
and opposable thumbs.
This power to touch with the tongue

and tell your beloveds,
the love of witnessing,

the greatness of what it means

to be the galaxies,

to be the stars,

to be the flower,

and to be the sun.

IT'S ALREADY HERE

Our soul's deepest desire is in our deepest longings. They aren't hungry. They are patient. They wait for the perfect moment to unfold.

Growing up, I was blessed with the belief that life is what you make of it. Yes, life happens to you, but you also have the power to shape your own reality.

I used to despise the word "manifesting" and the whole concept surrounding it. It felt unfair, especially for those genuinely impoverished and lacking privilege. Yet, I often find myself on the receiving end of unexplainable gifts.

I could sit here and justify how I've endured my fair share of hardship, wanting to prove that I'm not just an entitled princess. But that would be exhausting and miss the point entirely. Instead, I yearn to live like the dandelions in full bloom, scattered gently by the wind.

Throughout my life, I've experienced moments when the things I longed for, my heart's deepest desires, seemed to materialize. But the painful discovery I've made is that it cannot come to be when we ache for something that isn't first already inside us.

I always wanted Micah to love me so passionately. And he did, in ways, like surprising me with a honeymoon trip to Paris by placing our itinerary in a jewelry box covered with little strips of paper saying "I love you because…." Yet, within a few months of marriage, all our wounds split open, and we just kept hurting each other. We wanted the other person to heal us, to love us. When really, we both needed to heal and love ourselves.

Dr. Chelsea Page, one of my incredible coaches, describes manifesting as desiring. This shift in perspective changes the conversation and brings forward a vital realization.

You see, desire is not about hunger, thirst, or a greedy pursuit that makes us feel like we'll perish without it. No. Desiring is a profound soul longing—an ache that exists beyond the boundaries of reality. It is capable of bringing the intangible into existence. It surpasses the realm of cells, transcends the air we breathe, outshines the stars, and exceeds the sun's power. Yet, it does not consume us until there's nothing left.

Desiring is a gentle, subtle nudge. It is an opening, sometimes felt in a deep ache when surfaced. This feeling is most evident in my relationship with my beloved Moon. I yearn for him deeply, wanting to spend every moment of every day together. However, life presents its obligations: jobs, children, chores, and everyday tasks. Yet, this ache to be with him remains, sometimes painful but not overwhelming to the point of destruction.

The days we spend apart do not shatter me. They don't crush me. Even if circumstances like death, time, traffic, or sick children were to keep us apart, I know I'll be alright, and our desire will endure. It may get temporarily set aside, but the moment we reunite, whether through physical touch or any connection at all, I feel him and am reminded of how much I genuinely desire him.

After experiencing a near-death moment through severe illness the winter after divorcing Micah, I felt this yearning profoundly. All I wanted was a thousand sunsets with Moon. Nothing else mattered.

No other desire or thought consumed me—just a thousand evenings holding hands, admiring this beautiful world we live in, both lost in wonder.

We had just spent nearly two weeks apart due to different travel and family holiday plans. With each day separate, my heart did not grow heavier as if I was missing a limb. But instead, my desire for him grew deeper, to race home into his arms and never wish to leave them. The pain of our separation did not make me want to cut off a piece of my life to be with him. Instead, it asked me to trust that he would return; trust that this desire to be together would come to fruition because we both wanted it.

After returning from his trip, we were slammed with fewer days together due to kids getting sick and soon me getting sick. Yet, it only made our desire to be together stronger, to see that this intimacy is worth pursuing, but it couldn't come at the cost of our girls or ourselves.

This intimacy with him, this longing to be close, is gradually unfolding. Steps are being taken, allowing us to spend more time together and merge our lives. It's a slow, gentle process filled with hope and flexibility.

In the middle of it all, we escaped to a place on the coast where we lavished ourselves in each other's skin, took moonlight strolls on the beach bundled up in our wool layers, and giggled until our bellies hurt. We keep running back to this deep connection; knowing it's here, in these moments together, we get to fully experience what we desire.

And I can't help but think that this is what true desires are—they don't devour us alive. They don't burn us from the inside if we don't attain them. We yearn for them with every fiber of our being, yet we hold them loosely, knowing that the right time and way will align. We trust that we will receive what we truly desire in the most divine manner.

We must focus on what we want and how it is molded into our

lives. Our perspectives determine our reality. If we focus on what we lack, we'll only notice the absence.

Living in abundance allows us to see abundance everywhere. However, this approach can feel controlling and overwhelming. It doesn't leave room for the ache, the sorrow of feeling distant from what we desire. We should grieve the distance we're experiencing, but take heart in knowing what we deeply long for is already inside us. We're all just learning how this idea of separation isn't real. Like time, it's a construct because the feeling of desire, the desire itself, is already right here inside us.

HOLDING FLIGHT

Alicia, with a white-dyed pixie cut and a kitty purring on her lap, asked me from across my Zoom screen, "I don't know how to take what I want and make it come. But I did it with this one thing. How do you do that?"

The words spilled out of me as I sat on my wooden chair with trees as my background. "You have to hold it first. Hold, then hold it again, and keep holding it. Keep holding it."

"Yes, I need to write that down. Keep holding it. Just hold it." Her eyes lit up like the North Star. We knew it all came together right then—she'd found her way home.

We always think we're lost, but in the end, we find out it has been waiting for us right here inside, deep, deep inside.

This magic trick we have together to shift each other, is why I've loved working with Alicia through coaching and meditation for the past six months. I watched her sprout, but really, we bloomed together.

The hardest lesson, which is simultaneously a miraculous lesson, too, is that I'm learning that it's not our fault. Not every thought is our own, not every worry or fear even. It certainly is not who we are. Most thoughts, in fact, are inherited and passed down, or culturally agreed upon.

Meanwhile, the greatest lie I was ever taught was that my mind was my greatest asset. God, these things are brilliant. They hold so much, but damn, this body has generated the most beautiful feelings and realities I've ever known. Yet, it was this same body I was told was betraying me.

It's the lies, this belief system, that our minds are superior and that the messages ingrained into our very DNA are the ones we have to believe. They are swallowed with a gulp, not out of desire but out of the pain they take to be digested. Yet somehow, too many of us keep swallowing, wondering why we've lost our will to speak, our desire to live, and find numbness better than feeling alive because at least that's passable.

But I don't want a barely sufficient life. I want a magical, fully alive one. I don't want to numb out my pain because if I do, I'll numb out every ounce of joy that is being held behind what just needs a voice. Pain shouts, and we quiet it. But what if we let it out? Really letting it rage as we listen to it for once, asking, "What do you need, my dear?" In the freedom of removing those chains, joy is always there, waiting to take her hand and say, "I see you."

I've been plagued with trying to find my own way back home. It has felt like trying on old shoes. They are tattered and worn. Some fit just right because I wore them for so long. They are dusty and a little brown, although they started off a different color. I still adore every last pair, but I've outgrown them.

As I've been stepping deep into my own sexuality, I'm discovering the hidden pleasures I was taught to cut myself off from by religion and culture; being a woman meant I had to be at the feet of pleasing men, my spouse, instead of myself.

Expectedly, I've often been numb, doing, and dwelling with my strong arm of power. "I can do so much. Let me show you how." I let the masculine energy in me do a lot that week. I needed some safety, so it came with doing a lot of it, trying to control this haunting feeling I often wrestle with inside me that declares, "We're not safe."

However, as I chased control, I missed her. This wild dandelion of my soul, the feminine energy in me, ready to bloom and be wished into a shooting star, scattered across to only become yet another wish over and over again. Desire sent. Desire received. Pleasure is the purpose of life, and I'll go to any grave happily on that platform over anything else. Yet, I was stuck in a program, believing I wasn't safe. I reached for control instead of staying in play.

I'm learning to step back from bouncing between masculine doing and feminine being. We're re-learning balance; not control, not frustration, but in harmony and play. The space in the middle is where both get to be—structure with the free.

Yet, in the pattern locked so deep within me, I had closed her off: my pleasure. And then, in a dream-like sequence, I began to safely unlock her again as I let my own female sexuality open with pure desire. She finally came; came out to play, giggle, ravish, and be in all she adores.

In my mind, I keep running away from him, from my masculine energy, from everything that might bring me to where I always wanted to go. I'm so used to the flight: the rejection of reality because it was never safe to stay.

But these words slipped out of me as I learned them from Dr. Chelsea Page. We must first hold the feeling. Our job is to hold the feeling of what we want, and that's how it comes.

Sitting back with my coaching student, I realized I declared these words as if I were engraving them on stone, not only for her but for me. We both needed to be reminded that it was already here, everything we ever wanted.

Hold it. Don't let it go. It's here, right inside your home, the perfect symphony of your life. Hold it. Stay. I promise with all I have, it will be better than you've ever known.

NO MORE GHOSTS

No more lies
of who you cannot be
because of some rule
you've made,
some decisions you've *created*,
a reality that isn't the one you want,
but the one you think you deserve.

What if you do deserve this burning fire
of your desire?

Dreaming isn't scary.
Becoming is what makes us ghost ourselves

Storyteller

STORIES BUILD THE BRIDGE BETWEEN US

YOU DESERVE TO EXIST IN THE OVERFLOW

I KEEP FINDING HER

In the deep shadows, where past and present entwine, I kept finding her–the little girl lost in that dark corner, clutching her knees, waiting for someone to notice her desperate need. I, uncertain of how to help, closed the door, avoiding the depth of her pain. Occasionally, I'd creek the door open and pull it shut, finding it too dark to enter.

But then, her screams grew louder, demanding my undivided attention. I didn't know how to help her, so I just held her.

For six years, I'd been cradling her fragility. That's when I started to get sick; first with rashes, then with full-body disabilities and endless untreatable diagnoses. Rashes erupted on every extremity as if I had leprosy. This severed the bond between me and Olea, my two-year-old daughter at the time, prematurely tearing us apart before we were prepared. It sent my body spiraling. Guided by physicians, I pushed my body with medications in a futile attempt to mend the unhealable spaces.

Yet, my body resisted.

She was forced beyond her limits throughout an abusive childhood beneath a pile of men called 'family,' who demanded my sub-mission and silence.

So, with a pill from another man known as "Doctor," I helplessly trusted. I swallowed the pills, promising relief soon.

I drowned myself in it for two years, witnessing my own unravel-ing. Meanwhile, Micah, my ex-husband who vowed to love me most, descended into self-destruction, drowning his pain in concealed alco-hol. Yet, I felt bound to him because we were supposed to last forever and make each other feel better. This horrific lie of a Christian marriage filled our home with codependency and trauma bonding. We became the fire pit he constructed in our backyard, now reduced to smoldering ashes; smearing the faded pages of what once was, memories mostly forgotten but lingering in the eyes of our creation, our daughter, Olea.

The events of that fourth of July before we had Olea, weighed heavy in my heart. Micah invited some of his co-workers over to celebrate. Everyone got wasted while I watched, knowing I didn't like the feeling of being so out of control. I saw his phone lying open with a text to one of his women co-workers, Cat, whom he had pre-viously wanted me to meet one day, as he claimed, "You and her love the outdoors, I think you'd get along."

I read the texts flashing through his opened phone, which laid haphazardly on the coffee table next to our 1990s pale, multicol-ored-striped couch that Micah inherited from his family, following us for the next four years.

Micah text read, "I really want to fuck you so badly tonight."

To which Cat replied, "You cannot do that to your wife. I'm sorry."

Fury boiled in me like a volcano with magma coursing through her veins for years. I walked over to him as I showed him the phone and said, 'Are you fucking kidding me?' his phone across the room. No man was going to treat me this way and ruin my 'holy' Christian marriage. So I decided, at that moment, we would work it out.

'Why did you do that? How could you? This isn't okay. You need to get help...' spewed while Micah was still inebriated. He cowered on the couch, curled up into a ball. After we both cooled down, I called our church group leaders and told them what was happening, and they recommended therapy. Micah followed, like the good little boy he was made to be by his mother: when a powerful woman told him what to do. Yet, in that moment, I became his mother, and he became every single man who told me not to tell anyone when they touched me, all of them—liars.

Looking back, I wish I would have left. I wish he stood up for himself and was honest about what he wanted, which wasn't me. But again, my ego was not going to let some horny twenty-year-old ruin her marriage which was supposed to be dignified and holy in 'God's eyes.' So I stayed for eight more years, too many.

Finally, I hold her close, my inner little girl and this young woman so hurt by the men who were supposed to love her the most. I've delved into the roots, searching for the points where everything went awry, uncovering the gaps in the soil where our growth stagnated. Now, we break new ground with the arrival of spring, blossoming at last. For so long, I believed I had to learn to bloom upside down, never able to rise upward.

But now, I realize it wasn't the weight of gravity. I am not a victim. I am a divine goddess.

My Moon, my new partner, whispers this truth into my ear daily. "You are the most incredible woman I've ever known." We are breaking the rules of time with sore cheeks and stomach butterflies.

There is how I get sparked by my mentors and every single soul who illuminates a forgotten truth within me and I, them. This is the magic of human connection we so often forget. We are the light. We are the messages of rippling waves. We'll never cease. We'll never pause. We'll keep pouring, crashing, glittering in the sun, sparkling, raining, drawing in and out.

This is the magic I whispered in my own inner child's ear. "Please don't give up. I know you're scared. You cannot glimpse beyond this room where you've always found solace with knees to chest and only your arms to hold you." I gently grasped her hand and guided her to stand, urging her to open the door. This time, I leave it ajar, for beyond the door she's been living behind lies a bright light. It's our glorious life awaiting us.

"It's beyond your wildest imaginings. Remember all those movies you cherished? All the tales ever told? Well, it's even more remarkable than that. Every single day, it's going to surpass your wildest dreams. Please, don't give up. Don't quit. Please don't slam your head against that bathroom floor as Micah tells you he wants to leave. Stay with me through the night as you drift away. Stay with me as you give life to Olea; let Micah's call for support hold you. This is going to be worth it. Every single moment."

She nodded, tears streaming from both our eyes, mingling with the drip of snot that only comes with grief relief. The knot in my throat urges a deep belly roar. I lock my gaze with hers.

"Now, it's time to use our voices. What we have to touch is important. I know you yearn for a plan, control, and safety assurance. Can you trust me? I've been building safety every day just so you can speak."

A MIRROR-ENDING WAR

"Damn, girl, you're so freaking beautiful."

The resonance of those words lingered in my mind as I stood before the mirror, caught in a moment of profound confidence. It was the first time I looked in the mirror and said those words to myself. Not because anyone told me I should practice that. Not because I'd witnessed a single soul ever do that in person. But because I felt it in one of the rarest times in my thirty-three years of life.

I didn't dwell there long, gazing back at the image that met my eyes. "Yeah," I thought as my lips curved into a smile. "We truly are."

With a swift motion, I pulled up my hair, collected my purse, and made my way out, destined for the grocery store.

There were no grandiose plans. There was no wild outfit on. There was no makeup done nor lover to meet. It was just me going about my life.

Curiously, my inner monologue had never been infested with a ferocious self-critic, unlike Micah, who harbored an unrelenting bully in his head. My inner voice mostly whispered. Micah grew up with a harsh voice from his mother, unlike mine, who was very quiet. My internal dialogue resembled a silent splattering of thoughts like "I cannot" and questions asking me constantly, "Have you done enough?"

It's not a matter of measuring the severity of different internal voices. My heart goes out to those haunted by a relentless inner critic, especially when it spills into their external interactions. My advice to those who cross our paths with hurtful words is a gentle but firm, "No, thank you." Then, a compassionate suggestion that they embark on a healing journey before their words find a place in our ears.

After the divorce, my reality had merged with the fantasies of my adolescence. The man of my dreams, Moon, had come into my life. In various forms, he appeared in my dreams since I was a teenager.

When I was younger, I kept this running document on my laptop. In it, I wrote, "One day, I want my husband to like football as a way to connect with dad. He has to be tall with dark brown hair and bright eyes. He has to have a last name that starts with an A." The list went on with silly things a fourteen-year-old wishes for in a boyfriend one day. But little did I know, he actually existed, despite how I settled for a version of him in Micah, the one without a last name beginning with A.

These faint fragments converged into an unscripted reality when I chose to release the remnants of my connection with Micah that summer after years of him stating he was tired of being married. Moon quickly appeared in my life as if we were waiting for each other after too many experiments gone wrong decades prior. We needed each one to get to that exact moment when our girls met at a park playing, and Olea asked to get their phone numbers to play again.

Daily, Moon shares with me a cadence of affection, adorations, compliments, and whatever else pops up in his head. At first, it felt good, and I wondered when this would stop. Is this just flattery that helps him win over women? I felt his bold confidence on our first date—a magnetic allure I willingly embraced after a decade of scarcity. He was sexy as hell, and I knew exactly what I was getting into.

Sitting before the Sellwood waterfront, we spent hours watching the summer sunset as we both crept closer to each other to the point that he was touching me, and I him. At one point, he came out and told me, "Some people find me charming."

I smiled and giggled deep in my belly, thinking, "Good lord, who is this man? I freaking love him already."

I knew at that moment if I was going to live a beautiful life, I'd let myself fall in love as many times as I wanted. And even if some would see his statement as a red flag, I ate up his confidence like I used to ask the cruise servers for sugar to go on my strawberries. He and I were professional charmers, using our power for good in the world.

Whereas Micah's compliments were rare throughout a decade of marriage, with Moon, I was drenched in them as if they were new glitter. Given enough time, I'd soon believe the words that were sparkling and sticking to my skin.

As the months passed with him, I understood that Moon's affections flowed freely to everyone. To his daughters daily, his family, his mother, his ex-wife, the garbage man he greets out front of his condo every Wednesday morning, and the volunteer staff at his daughters' school evening events. This is just who he is. If he feels the adoration, he will boil over like a shouting kettle telling you all how he's wholeheartedly feeling.

Eight months in, his showering affections changed my own inner whisper. As I stand looking in the mirror with my daughter, I often tell her, "You are so beautiful. I love your round tummy and how amazing of a kid you are!"

My daughter looks at herself in the mirror with fun, play, and joy. And I hope nothing ever changes for her in that.

She often asks me as we cuddle in bed before sleep, "What's your favorite color?"

It's been green most of my life, but then Moon told me his favorite color was bubbles, I thought, what a brilliant idea. Who said your favorite color couldn't be a thing holding color? So, mine soon became the ocean because that is all my favorite colors.

One evening, pretending to play puppies with Olea on the floor, wrestling, and drinking water from a bowl on the laminate-looking wood, I told her, "Your eyes are my favorite color."

She blushed and replied with her usual eight-year-old tone, "Mommmyyyyy." We giggled and resumed our game.

I want her to adore every inch of herself, to know what being proud feels like, and not look to others to find out if she's beautiful but stare straight in the mirror and know it in her bones.

This self-adoration wasn't part of my own upbringing. Yet, fueled by my tenacity to foster it in Olea, healed by Moon's unwavering affection, and positive online communities of nurturing, candid conversations with friends, I sense a tide of healing rippling over me and out past myself. After decades of not knowing this could be my existence, I'm finally declaring truth over myself, as if I'm declaring victory after a thirty-year-long war.

"Damn, girl, you're so freaking beautiful."

MAKING LIVES BEAUTIFUL

My thumb lived in my mouth most of my childhood, the soothing ache to hold in my truth that bent the top of my mouth for twelve years. Pastes, threats, and warnings never deterred me. It wasn't until someone with kindness offered something better.

"Do you want straight teeth and a beautiful smile?"

I looked him in the eyes, straight through the lens of his glasses as the incandescent lighting shone straight into mine with my head tilted back in the dentist's chair.

I loved to make people smile by smiling at them. Deep in me, I knew if I could make my smile brighter, it would make everything else brighter, too. I remember walking along city streets with my family, holding my mother's hand, staring across the street at strangers, just smiling. Seeing how they would go from glooming serious faces to vivid and full of life just because I smiled at them.

With hovering lights over my head and squinted eyes, I nodded in a resounding, "Yes." Please give me those metal bricks inside my mouth, and I'll stop with the comfort of this appendage, my thumb.

I wanted more radiance to spread further than I wanted the comfort of my thumb in my mouth.

One spring afternoon, my daughter and I drove from our studio apartment to her dad's home. She'd been asking many questions about whether certain things would make her daddy happy. I kept reminding her it wasn't her job to make him happy. I wanted too badly to unravel these lies our genealogy had made us believe: that we're responsible for others' emotions. But I just learned this. It became a whole new thing to teach my seven-year-old. Yet I knew how hard it was to be around him when he was sad. All you want to do is just make him smile. His energy of sadness drains the room, along with you in it like a kiddy pool without its plug. It can feel impossible not to become emptied yourself.

She said from the back seat, "He doesn't laugh very much except when I tickle him." She giggled at the end, and I felt her head tilt as it always does when she's shyly satisfied with herself.

I laughed at the thought. Micah hated to be tickled, but it quickly elicited a full-body giggle.

We made cookies the night before just for fun. And before we got ready to drive her to her dad's house, she asked if we could bring him some.

A few days later, Olea came home delightedly and declared, "Daddy was happier after he had the cookies we made. Then he played Playdough with me!"

She helped bring him joy. And she lit up like the lightbulb we had just switched on as the sun began to set outside our apartment window.

During our drive to his house with cookies in tow earlier, our conversation continued, and I said, "It's beautiful you want to make daddy happy even though it's not your job."

And then this wisdom spilled out of her seven-year-old mouth, divinity dripping from the ruby of her lips, "That's what you love to do for people too, Mommy. You and I, we like to make people's lives beautiful."

The road became slightly blurry, and I knew I couldn't let the river of tears flow out of me. So, I responded only with the facts.

"I'm so proud to be your mommy. You are such an amazing kid." I affirmed as I reached back to tenderly squeeze her hand, a small gesture I wanted to express with my whole body in the flood of my own pride.

"I know." I felt her smile. The one where she tilts her head to the left, raises her left shoulder to greet her cheek as the right shoulder curls in and her lips spread while her eyelashes flutter.

I reached back for her hand and gave it the squeeze I wanted to express with my whole body.

I may not have been able to be her full-time mommy as she left the comfort of her cribbed bed a year too early. But if this is her passion, her mission; as she seeks to make her friends giggle with her "old lady bit," grabbing a nearby stick, pretending to be an old lady as she changes her voice asking for help. She's always the one to check on her classmate who isn't doing well.

One day, she came home to tell me about a classmate she wasn't close to who was bleeding. She noticed no others were checking on him, so she went to see if he was okay. But soon, the teacher arrived to care for him. Over and over again, she is always looking for ways to love people.

She's the one who will often leave love notes throughout the house. Nothing more than a cute drawing, and her forever flipped writing that says:

"I love you.
From: Olea.
To: Mommy"

I'm too in love with her expression of needing to be seen because she sent it to you instead of needing it to be correct. Because when she shares this with me, she needs to be seen and loved in return.

Fast forwarding to the beginning of the pandemic, I found myself on the kitchen floor, weeping for all the people dying so quickly. Instead of asking me what was wrong or trying to cheer me up, she quietly came and brought me one of her favorite stuffies and hugged me.

She is the anchor for caring for others. She knows how my mother and grandmother taught me this in childhood. She forever witnessed this. And maybe it's been passed down in the energies of women who have only known trauma bonding and abuse. Make them happy so you can find peace: my mother and grandmother taught me only this. It appeases everyone around you so you can have inner peace. It's not until you appease everyone else that you can be okay.

Oh, but not us. We're taking this superpower and spreading it to the world. We get to turn darkness into light, not just brightness for sad partners.

We'll touch every person we pass by with our radiance. For me, it started with my straight teeth. And with Olea, it's been in all the ways she loves. And I'm doing everything in my power to hold us both sacred.

As we both grow together, I will witness her being the anchor for caring for others. I'll keep saying "yes" to more vibrancy and luminosity as we become the headlamps in this world that can sometimes seem like a forever night.

HARVESTING S T A R S

To describe the power of the weakest point she'll ever be is like trying
to harvest stars in your living room chandelier.

It is absolutely absurd.

Which is why I think you should at least,
once in your lifetime,
go stand in front of something **fierce**.

Just so you can *remember* what it's like,
to remember you're also here to powerfully create.

UNEARTHED

I feared for my safety, haunted by the memories of past men who had hurt me. Would he inflict the same pain? Would his words, which seemed true, deceive me like others before; tearing my heart apart with contradictory actions?

But he's different—he's unlike any of them. Still, I remain on the hunt to protect myself, proclaiming daily, "This will not happen again."

Dating Moon after divorcing Micah opened so much in me, especially as I built safety back inside my body.

Safety is a sensation that must first take hold within our bodies. In my case, it feels like the slow drip of fresh concrete being poured. Instead of drying, it keeps raining inside my subconscious, wondering when we'll know solid.

The sun emerges time and time again, prompting me to wonder if today will be the day. Can we maintain our shape without everything slipping away?

Finding balance is crucial, especially regarding dating and managing separate lives.

It's like juggling wobbly jello molds while walking a tightrope as others (especially those of my past) imaginarily shout their opinions about my life. The echoes of my own history and self-judgment reverberate in my mind, whispering, "This isn't right."

A part of me yearns to knock it all down and run away. But escaping into solitude only invites judgments and lies to dwell deeper within. There is no escape; it would merely serve as a distraction.

So, here I sit; purging my thoughts onto paper, knowing that when I release them from my body, they remain here—rather than clinging to my lungs. They resemble the phlegm of a recurring bacterial infection. To eradicate them permanently, I must expel and devour them with the power within me. That's my dedicated pursuit, as much as I can bear.

It's an exhausting process, and a part of me resists, beckoning, "Don't leave." We've been intimately intertwined for so long that it's difficult to discern whether a part of me is leaving or if it's just the lies I've been breeding.

Yet, with each purge, I feel lighter in my being. The heaviness in my chest diminishes, and my smile shines brighter.

It took a storm to uproot every fiber of my being, a side of healing rarely spoken of. It involves finding new roots and discovering fresh soil. It goes beyond merely shedding the weight of the past. It's about unearthing, replanting, and genuinely understanding what it means to feel at home. But only by lifting the foundations and uncovering the depth of the rot can we create our own fertile soil; transcending into the realm of our soul's beckoning. There is always much more to experience than what we've settled for.

You are the breaker of cycles, the conqueror of the evolution of your blood, your tribe, your people, and your soul. It won't be easy, demanding your utmost dedication. But it will become the greatest accomplishment of your life.

I stand beside you, unearthing and replanting. Reminding myself that safety is the feeling I create in this precious body. Meanwhile,

I thank fear for reminding me that I am alive. But now, it's time to stand tall in my power, knowing that I reign supreme over every aspect of my existence.

I MET AN OWL TODAY

Owls are believed to carry the dead to the afterlife and are some-times seen as omens of death. One evening, as I walked through the forest behind my apartment, I began to go back home through the rain and darkening night. Draped in my waterproof winter jacket, boots, and rain pants, I squished through the damp soil, meandering back down the hill of the volcano lined with a wealth of growth; carpeted with ferns, evergreens, and leafing trees, moss dripping off them all. A deep chill ran through my bones as I heard the hoot of an owl in this forest for the first time. It added to the weight I had already carried within me. The darkening night hugged me with the heaviness I had already felt in my blood. I had just confronted battles that once felt impossible to wage. These battles, stored deep in my cells, were now released during this doctor-suggested cleanse I embarked on, marking the third day of consuming only bananas and spinach. This pattern of walking through the forest often soothes me when I'm profoundly processing myself. Still, that night reminded me of a truth I'd yet to discover.

I slept until half past eight, the longest I had slept in for a quarter of the year, perhaps even since I had parted ways with Micah just six months before. The decade-long relationship that was the toxic ink tattooed to my cheek, "You're not enough," a lie I believed when I was with him. Every conversation he had to push me away, repeated in my subconscious like a broken record. "I'm not sure I want to be with you," had morphed into my head as I was not enough. Over and over, this etched itself into my cells until it became a part of me, making it increasingly difficult to combat the toxins in my blood caused by the unhealthy food I consumed, mainly processed foods and an excessive amount of chocolate. The ongoing argument of whether our addictions were our cure or our demise, persisted. Still, now I knew that neither option was supporting my compromised cells.

On this day, the cleanse that my doctor had suggested consisted of bananas and spinach. "Why don't you try it and see how you feel each day?" she had advised. Her guidance echoed through the pages of the books that accompanied me on this journey. These cleanses were meant to release the stored messages my body had once held. Unable to process what was happening to me in real-time, my cells held them for me. But now, with this cleanse, it aided every last memory, message, and truth to be released.

My body sheltered them. It replied, "We have too much going on. So we're placing them in this beautiful box right here. We'll place the lid on so they don't fight. I know those clothes are now tight, but please trust us. We're trying to keep you alive."

Containment theory was one of the methods my therapists taught me. It is where you place your emotions and situations inside a metaphorical container until you're ready to pull out the memories and safely deal with them, instead of feeling like they are hungry monsters about to eat you alive. It's with this same idea that I've surrendered to my body's process of gaining weight as I healed myself from the trauma bonding of my past relationship with Micah, seeing how it wasn't just a pattern with him but a pattern with every single person in my life up until this point. That is, until I met Moon.

Before him, each person I was close with was always playing the victim and the other the rescuer. My parents tried to keep me quiet about the abuse, and with things going wrong under the surface as the victim, they always provided me with money when they didn't do the same with my sister. They paid for my college while she drowned in student loans; working a part-time job while I got to travel to New Zealand on a mission trip.

Then, there was my best friend, Billie, who would call me any-time she felt remotely alone. We had the absolute most fun together; staying out late, going to concerts, hanging out with cute boys, being ridiculously silly, and dressing up in fun outfits. We lived inside our own montage of our eighteen-year-old selves. However, Billie would often randomly ghost me and not answer phone calls or text messag-es for days. But when other people got close to me, or said they had a crush on me and wanted to ask me out, she would convince them that we weren't a good fit because they would take up space carved out for her in my life.

Then, of course, there was Micah, whom I tried to mother; be-lieving that if only I could love him so well, he'd come to give me the love I deserved. Each time, we all tried to control the other to get our needs met. This was what my body was finally ready to release.

Having laid in bed longer than usual, I was reluctant to face the world. Tears welled up in my throat, yet they refused to appear in my eyes. But as I continued to delve into my thoughts and emotions, a wellspring of grief bursted out, transforming into a fountain of emo-tions. Overwhelmed, I sought solace in the confines of my bathtub, uncertain whether I would ever breathe fresh air again.

Returning to my bed an hour later, I allowed the tears to flow freely until my bed became a sea of tissues outnumbering the pil-lows. I yearned for this agony to subside, wondering why I hadn't yet emerged as a whole being, as the sheer volume of tissues suggested based on my past experiences of letting my body feel all the feelings that I would, by now, be ready to move on.

With nothing left to nourish my empty belly, I remained in bed, propped up awkwardly on my side, cradled by my pink pillow, and covered by a blanket up to my neck. At that moment, I resorted to the only thing I knew how to do—I dove into my subconscious. I embarked on a journey within, using various meditation techniques such as rotating my awareness, practicing mental alternate nostril breathing, and envisioning symbols that guided me to the depths of my consciousness. These slow brain waves, sought after when we are told to sit still, close our eyes, and empty our minds, led me to a different exploration. It allowed me to discover the opposite of emptiness, the voice of my inner guide.

She unveiled the depths and the battles I had been fighting, and the actions I had believed I must face alone. I sincerely thought that I couldn't be in relationships anymore; that I had to be alone. Because if I was, I would just trauma bond again. I'd play the roles I was taught to play and end up in endless cycles of chaos and misplaced control.

I wept, convincing myself that I needed to isolate myself, even from the glorious new presence in my life—Moon, who had recently arrived. I convinced myself that I must leave him behind, fearing that the weight of my struggles would be too much to bear, let alone burden him with. So, I wept, believing that perhaps the death of us was the only escape.

However, as I delved deeper into my meditation visions, I saw myself sitting before a familiar place on the ocean cliffs, my favorite spot on the Oregon coast. The grass was forever green there, and whales would often gather while crashing waves danced along the edge of the rocks. Haunted whispers of untold time, of questioning reality, mingled with the infinite continuity of infinity itself. I watched it all unfold, holding my knees tightly, allowing the waves to carry my seemingly endless grief.

And then, as if the sun rose again, warmth enveloped me—a pair of legs wrapped around me. Sometimes, in my meditations, this sensation represented an older version of myself coming to my rescue. Still, I didn't feel the need to be saved this time. Instead, I longed for a comforting embrace, a reassurance that I was not alone in this tumultuous journey. I didn't have to swim through the depths of my emotions unaccompanied. It was then, in my visions, Moon with his lengthy legs cradled me in his arms offering solace. I felt a sense of warmth, and the loneliness I hadn't recognized before dissolved. The vision shifted to where I was climbing a rope, and I could hear Moon cheering me on. "You've got this, babe. Hang on tight. I'm right here, rooting for you!"

At the same time, my inner guide assured me, "You can do this, but you don't have to do it alone. Allow the radiance of others to assist you in your ascent. You are not dependent and won't succumb to the bonds of trauma again. Strength lies in accepting support sometimes. So, hold on tightly and lean on him when you need that extra boost to reach the relief of the summit."

I emerged from this meditation experience feeling relieved and filled with joy. I had initially thought I had given my trust to Moon, believing he would be my source of safety, just as I had once done with Micah. But it dawned on me that this belief had been an illusion concocted by fear, an attempt to sabotage and isolate myself, allowing the shadows to consume me whole.

Returning to the reality of my bed, where the messages that had once burdened my cells shattered and dissipated. I do not need to be rescued to be loved. I do not need to be a victim to be provided for. I am worthy of love for just being alive. Abundance exists in every fiber of my cells and all I touch with this knowing is truth.

But something in me still needed release. So, I reached for charcoal sticks to express what words alone couldn't hold. Covering the page full of charcoal, I began here by taking out instead of adding in. The page that had started with darkness was gradually transformed, creating negative space—a representation of my current journey. My black page turned into a storm, a sign, and a darkened sun. I didn't fully comprehend their meaning. However, I left them on the page as a message for my future self:

We can navigate the depths, even when unsure which way is up. We won't drown in these waters of deep emotions and past patterns. Ride the currents of the tides, freely knowing we're in the flow of our choosing. And most importantly, we don't have to face our struggles alone. I finally let my head hit the pillow, allowing the earth to embrace me and remind me that warmth is best felt when shared with others, not just one solitary figure lost in time.

The owl I'd heard earlier that night wasn't the death of this new relationship; it was discovering the death of the lies that said I had to be alone—the end of isolation. So I clung close to this new man, teaching me how to be a survivor of trauma, knowing the safety of pure love that wants nothing of you but your existence with them. Rebirthed, I emerged as someone capable of holding such truths. And I pay my respects to the owl who reminded me of the beauty of death's reincarnation, which we can experience multiple times in this life.

THE EXIT OF EARNING LOVE

Boom, boom, the throbbing, heart-pumping beat. This way must not go on. As it beats like a nervous actress, the tempo of my heart paces her steps, fearing the audience will not adore them. My heart has been in survival, trying its best to keep up with the demands of conditional love—the belief that affection is exchanged for action, a performance on a stage of expectations. I've found a new way, how we don't earn our love.

Exiting stage right, I must exit the show I was told to perform. But now, I'm on the sidelines, waiting for Act Two to begin. It has no script. So I'm improvising. Every inch of me is stepping into the unknown. How do I let my body dwell in adoration when it has only known affection in exchange?

Exploration is the wisest place to find new discoveries, but it's also where anything and everything is possible. I'm here on this landing rim. The audience is waiting, leaning at the edge of their seats. Something in the air fills their lungs with the cue of our flesh to raise the hairs on end. Anticipation. Leave it unresolved, and it turns to terror. But hold it long enough to end with marvel, and you've touched pure joy.

This is the act I'm stepping into with sheer terror and utter delight for what I know will be the closing curtain.

I've only known love with strings attached. My father taught me this repeatedly when execution needed to be the knife to which he cut his own bloodline out. But because he didn't, the bravery is now mine. It has all ended with me. No more sacrificial love. No more trying to earn someone's love by being good enough for them.

I lied weeping on Moon's shoulder on our now shared back patio, as the sun kissed us both. Even she knew how to love us without our efforts.

Moon and I had been caught up in another disagreement, our lifestyles differing wildly from how we had raised our girls. Yet, after every conflict, he comes back, grabbing both of my hands and says, "I'm in this with you. We're a team in this."

I retract and go inside. I've never had someone want to fight for something with me instead of against me. I always thought it was about having to fight to be right, but Moon teaches me a new way to love: to stand together as a team, to find understanding, and sometimes even agree to disagree.

Sitting curled up on my yoga mat on the patio as he comes out to hug me after I meditate, I reply to him, "I don't deserve your love. I know I do. We all do. But I don't feel as if I'm good enough."

In his quipped reply, "I don't feel like enough for you either. Maybe we should lower our standards."

My solemn face turns upwards with a smile, and I laugh. There's a relief we get after feeling at different ends trying to find the middle together. But really, we were on the same side, just still looking for the middle of the same rope.

We both turn our sorrow into joy. This is the magic of laughter.

How do you let yourself be loved just for being alive when you've only known love as an exchange for all you can do for someone?

What do you do to find love? What do you do to be loved? You breathe. You exist. You are. Therefore, you are loved.

What if the greatest truth isn't that we don't have all we want, because it's already here. We just aren't ready to know it yet. The cells in our bodies are programmed to believe, to live as if it's not true.

Mine have only known flight. I've done quite well. I'm here. I'm alive. I've shifted as I nailed these lies to the cross to be crucified. Knowing the real meaning of this story was to teach us, "You are everything. We are all one. Love. Infinite. Holy. Divine. Enough."

But don't you see, it's not that you don't know this. It is why you weep when you hear those words. It's written in your humanity. But in the line passed down, living with these bodies, we reject it. We behave as if it's not the truest thing as the sun sets each day. Will you come to recalibrate?

I've spent too long rejecting the truth of my body, telling my pain it just needed to be quiet. In all reality, it was the very pain that was trying to show me a piece of me that had been lost, forgotten, and needed only my gentle hand of affection to rescue her from all the wrong she endured.

Stepping bravely again as my hands shake and my legs feeble, I'll come to stand with you on this stage in the Second Act. We no longer subscribe to the belief that our worth is found in our accomplishments. Acting as solid links, we'll hold hands and rest our heads on each other's shoulders every single day until every last cell in us believes the truth in our hearts beats: we are love, infinite, endless, and worthy.

COTTON GLACIER

Hold me close for alone, it's frigid.
Autonomy with matrimony.
How do you marry the self with another
and keep the two,
not as one but in their own divinity?

Self-identifying.
Reaching out to support without leaning against each other.
The gentle mirror to hold up when a hand is too weak
to see the beauty already within.

Is that the true power?
Misguided to be used as a crunch
until we find how to stand upright?

Yet, this affection is not that simple.
It is adoration, admiration, pure desire, and delight in another.

The touching of every moment,
knowing how none can be grasped
because the other is your favorite dessert.
The ice cream bound to melt,
but cannot be frozen for later
because the melting must saturate to exist in the river,
into the clouds,
into the snow,
into the glaciers,
into the ocean,
where it will become more significant than itself.

So, hang on to every kiss of your lips
and this reminder that it's all so sweet,
and we mostly experience what we choose to taste.

Paradoxically, I sit here alone.
Needing to calm the storms inside
when all I want to do is float
in the clouds,
in the snow,
in the glaciers,
in the ocean,
and let it devour every inch of my skin.
I want to be that ice cream glacier river,
make it my undertone,
pink and red sandwiched with the sun.

Kiss me good day, and let me go pl a y !

But I'm in no water.
This bed has gotten comfortable,
but I no longer want cotton.

I want this liquid gold
beaming through my window.

My doctor tells me to stay away,
or it will add to the viral load.
This vessel cannot handle it anymore.
The skin has pickled on my hand,
there is a rumble in my lungs,
jelly in my throat, spiraling out my nose,
and pain in my root.
It all must anchor me here to this cotton belly.

So maybe I'll become a tree instead of the fish I'm aching to be.
Dwell right by the water,
so my roots can still drink of her,
this cloud-made snow-covered glacier,
pouring into the ocean that's calling me as I try to remember.
Our love can exist outside of the prescribed
math being placed on us from all the old stories.
I know we're here to melt them back into the earth.

LEARNING ADDITION TAKES TIME

Every night, I share a precious moment with Olea in the bed I now share with Moon. This time is especially significant for her, as she learns to adjust to sharing my attention with three other family members in our newly blended family.

My stepdaughter Maddie, has also started coming to our bed recently. Her dark brown hair was freshly washed and pulled into a ponytail. She pounces onto the bed and curls up with a blanket next to us as quickly as she enters. I touch her forehead as she tells me stories of her day. Maddie quickly jumps out of bed and says goodnight as she walks to the girls' shared bedroom.

When Maddie was in the sixth grade and attended an emotionally challenging school, we hit a peak moment. Maddie would often come home with short sentences and struggled to express herself without sarcasm or childish facial expressions. She can be like a yin and yang, sometimes unsure of which side you'll get, it can feel exhausting. But when I look into her eyes, I see so much of myself in her.

Unknowing how to handle the overwhelm of life, it was through controlling my environment that I created some semblance of peace. I became the one always making my bed. When Olea was born, and I felt the most unsafe after our traumatic delivery, I became obsessed with the cleanliness of our floors. I would wash our dog's paws regularly and refuse to let him lick Olea anywhere. Olea had to be bathed daily, even if we never left the house. Whenever I've felt chaos around me, I find myself trying to control the places where I exist and often people, too.

It's been challenging for Maddie and Jean to express themselves safely and healthily. We often label this behavior as "X age going on sixteen." But what if we normalized children who knew how to express themselves and adults who knew how to do the same? It could change our world. I've been advocating for this in our new blended family: normalizing feelings and learning safe expressions while honoring them. However, it hasn't been easy, and sometimes I find myself avoiding Maddie and Jean as if they aren't the gems I know they are, simply because I feel helpless about how to help them.

I had promised myself that when we got married, I wouldn't take responsibility for teaching these girls a lifetime of lessons while I was barely beginning my relationship with them as their "bonus mom." I didn't want to be their therapist.

Until one day, I finally belted out to my husband, "I cannot tolerate this anymore. This behavior has to stop. These girls need support."

We spiraled, and he came undone. I did my best to try not to let this dictate our future.

Deep in my body, I feared unkind talk from childhood, as I did from my father. My promise to keep myself safe flared and I did the only thing I remembered to do: don't be home, stay in your room, and don't talk to anyone.

As a child, I'd hide away from my family, go to neighbors, find myself consumed in every social activity school could offer, or find every excuse to be gone.

I pulled apart, and it left the ache in all of us. Loneliness can

settle quickly, even in a household of five, until I burst. We turned.
I communicated as best I could. My husband took it with so much
grace, despite the weight it held for him. He struggled not to let the
internal stories dictate: fearing he failed them and that they were not
safe for Olea and me.

But none are true. These are only fears that keep us from having
the desired life. Like I believed was my greatest power while shutting
my childhood bedroom door.

I used to slam it in rebellion to my dad's volatile outbursts. I was
scolded by him every time. Yet, this separation was the only way I
knew how to keep myself safe. But we are not children anymore. We
are the parents. So I knew I could not hide again behind the rectan-
gles of coffin-shaped hinges where I imagined separation begins.

The next day, we spent it mostly apart. Moon had conversations
and did his homework to get more support in teaching his kids to
emotionally regulate themselves in late adolescence.

Jean and Maddie shared their pieces with him, and he listened to
how it's been hard for them to have another sister who is so different
and processes in dissimilar and frustrating ways.

We met and talked. And the moment Olea and I returned home
from our separate outings, Jean, ready to fashion show their new store
finds, greeted me. Our night resumed like there was no war raging.

Still, it was just our beautiful blended family coming together as if
we weren't separate colors in different containers—but watercolors on
watercolor paper being made into something new.

Bedtime looked different after this. Olea came to cuddle me
before bed, along with Maddie and Jean. Then Maddie crawled in,
puckered her heart-shaped lips, and kissed me on the forehead.
"You're the second person that's not my blood family I've kissed." She
rolled next to me with the blanket pulled up to her chin, laying on
her side, eye to eye with me.

"Oh...tell me who the other one is?" My heart froze in time of
what this meant. Her deep love for me, the one I feel so undeserving

of, but will gladly accept as we learn how to grow together.

"A boy in kindergarten..." She told me the story to which the details filtered out of me as Jean curled up next to me, interlacing her fingers with mine, smashing her face so our noses could wiggle together.

I cling to these little big moments. Knowing with each day, each month, and each year, we'll get better at knowing how to go from two and three to five—learning addition takes time.

STICKY-RICED SOCKS

With their rainbow-dyed bobbed haircut, Jean came home from school early in pain; having had a hard day with a violent classmate and another not respecting their physical boundaries. Over and over, it seems unkindness is replicated as their way of life in their school. And what are we but giant mirrors to the environments in which we exist?

Sympathy is a bit like syrup. If its intentions are sweet, it is soothing. If it's cold, it'll sting. And if it's out of obligation, it will feel more like cooked rice on the bottom of your feet after their pieces have lost their way to the floor from tabletop mouths: sticky and utterly annoying. I tried my fair share of well-intended syrups, apologizing for their bad day at school but ultimately holding my emotional shield up high. I didn't want to get too close because part of me still felt afraid this wouldn't work out somehow. But I made a vow and will do my best to keep this one.

Nonetheless, I was half there in the affections I would have had if it were my own flesh and blood coming home with the same complaints. I would have smothered like a fierce mama bear, demanding justice and weeping with them.

But I'm only half a step down of a mom to them, my Jean. I've only known them for a year, living together a quarter of that time, as Moon and I co-parent with Jean and Maddie's mom.

I cannot say which school they attend or talk to their teachers about the bullies. I cannot rescue them to the Waldorf school my Olea attends. I'd been to those schools, and I was probably that bully who was lying and cheating, hitting in my rage of not knowing how to regulate my emotions, with all the big feelings I felt from the horrific things happening at home that no one knew about.

So I kept silent and stepped in only when Jean asked to play my meditation games, do kid yoga, dance together, or shepherd them to pick up Olea at school. I fill my role as I learn to be a bonus mom with what sometimes feels like little influence.

Dinner was made, and all of us were fed. Jean left the table without doing their one evening chore: putting their dishes in the dishwasher. Overwhelmed by unregulated emotions, they gave us a snarled look when asked to put them away. Reluctantly, they put their dishes away and then plopped themselves back down on the couch, seemingly lifeless. These behaviors match their sister Maddie's when she, too, feels overwhelmed and out of control.

From the recesses of the couch, Jean proclaimed they wanted a pet, a plant, or something. In annoyance at the disrespectful facial expressions and infuriating behavior of being asked to do one chore, I replied as I began washing the dishes, "Maybe if you show us you're responsible enough to put away your dishes without complaint, we can."

Returning to the table to finish my dinner, I joked that it was a lot to chew as smoothies have been many of my meals lately with my health. I laughed out loud at how silly it was to have a sore jaw just from chewing a big bowl of salad.

Jean chuckled in mockery. I felt the blood rush to my face at the end of my fuse. My eyes grew wide, and I wondered what my Moon would do. His eyes grew laser-focused on Jean with a look of disappointment and disapproval, communicating in ways only parents of years with their offspring can. I calmly said, "Jean, did you mean to make fun of me? That wasn't very nice." They shrugged and gave a sticky-riced sock apology.

I took a deep breath and finished cleaning up the dishes. Olea had begun to wonder about playing a game and asked me to join while Jean stomped up the stairs, Moon following after them.

A few minutes later, I heard Jean crying loudly from the bedroom they shared with Maddie and Olea. A large piece of me wanted to run up, crawl into bed with them, apologize for not being more tender and patient, and ask why they had such a horrible day. Instead, I only offered my sticky-riced sock and turned my head the other way.

In reality, I let my mind wander in the whisper I regret even feeling, "Will this ever get better? Will this continue and be the end of our new blended family? These girls, and the anger they experience daily, within not knowing how to regulate themselves and deal with their lives is a lot. And I wonder, will I be able to handle the next implosion."

I daydreamed for a moment of two houses separate but still married. Maybe it would be better. Being in the brunt of all these big emotions seems so hard. I shook my head as if to declare that we cannot even imagine such a thing. We are here. We made our promises, the sweet, syrup-soothing kind.

Within moments, Moon, with red-flooded eyes, asked me to come upstairs to their room. Jean was curled in bed, and Moon asked if I could snuggle with them.

Immediately, I went upstairs and climbed into bed with Jean. As their whole body wept with grief, they said, "I'm sorry for making fun of you." An all too familiar feeling, where breath cannot match the grief you feel, so it shortens like a staccato. You wonder if it's here that you'll end right with an exclamation mark, unable to catch your breath.

Mama Bear mode turned on, and I took deep breaths. I know how to be strong for my beloveds. I took a deep breath with my hand resting on Jean. They matched for a moment, then slipped back to their grief-filled staccato. I asked them if they wanted to try something Olea and I do when we feel heaps of emotions. They nodded their head in agreement.

Calmly, I asked, "What color or colors do you see with what you're feeling?"

Quickly, they replied, "Green."

"Okay, what texture does it have: bumpy, lumpy, round, smooth?"

"Lumpy, dark green."

"Where do you feel it in your body?"

"In my tummy."

"Okay, what would you like to do with the lumpy dark green feeling in your tummy? Do you want to keep it there? Do you want me to take it out of you? Do you want to put it somewhere?"

"Take it out."

"Okay. Where do you want to put it?"

"In the trash."

"Okay, let's slam dunk that in the trash."

They moved their hands with their eyes closed. We'd been practicing this, already letting our imaginations hold space for us in an Orb meditation game we've played most nights where we pretend to put our feelings, a memory, or sensation inside a ball that we pass to the person next to us just for fun. Having practiced this before, Jean dropped in and immediately saw that their emotions were just that: emotions. They didn't have to have a word, but instead it could have a form, one in which they could choose to be the author of. Goosebumps filled me as I felt the truth. "No, this is my role. I cannot control, but I can guide. I can support you. I can be a voice when everything else feels dark."

I can see who I am as their bonus mom in moments like these. This is the gift of witnessing them all, being supportive when life is overwhelming because I've wrestled my own demons and know how to tame each one, learn if they have a voice, silence if they hold a lie, and let go once they have served their purpose. I'll be here when they need to hold the space of sweet syrup and remind myself to remove my socks when they get too sticky with rice inside my ragged, safety control box of coping mechanisms.

DIFFERENCES ARE YOUR MAGIC

I whispered into her ear,
"Your differences are your *magic*."

North Star

WE FIND OUR
WAY HOME BY
REMEMBERING
OUR TRUE SELVES

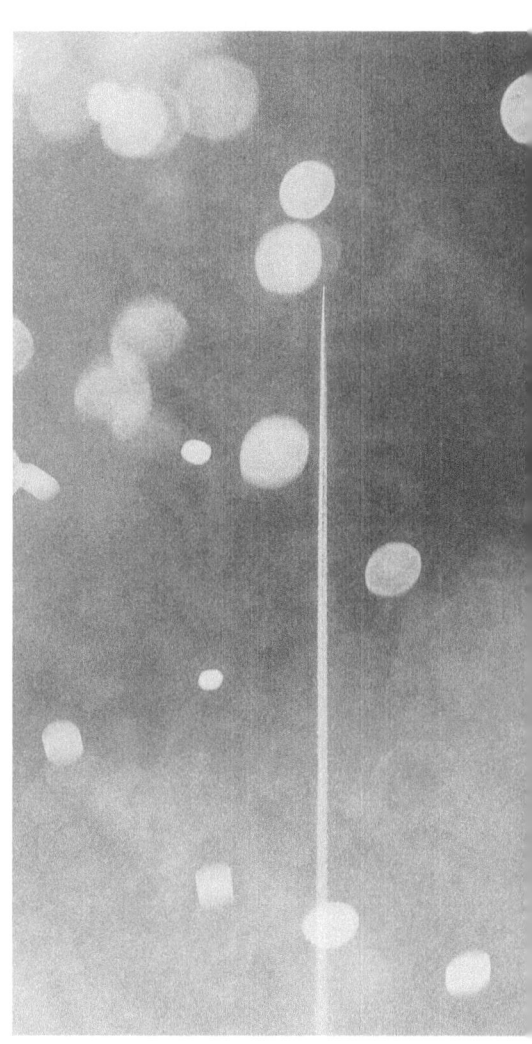

WE ARE NOT THE STORIES WE WERE TOLD

SHE CAME TODAY

The wise woman in me, with her long silver hair that blew with the wind as she stood on the edge, embodied the brilliance of a lighthouse. Her roots granted her power, and she fearlessly declared her truth on this day.

Two important people asked too much of me in one fell swoop, and for the first time, I did not collapse. It was a spring day, with tulips beginning to bloom while the sun graced us with an extra hour of warmth amid the Pacific Northwest rain. When I stepped into this woman, I knew I could be her. Finally, her shoes fit perfectly. They used to ache as I grew, but now they feel just right.

Micah had asked for a meeting to discuss and reflect upon the past six months of our separation and divorce. We were to delve into the depths of where we had been and the trials we had faced; and how, in the blink of an eye, twelve years had condensed into mere seconds, shaping us into the individuals we are today.

We met at a cozy coffee shop near the 300-square-foot studio apartment where Olea and I resided, nestled against my beloved park in Portland, before we blended families with Moon. I walked in to find Micah in line about to order. We calmly stood in line, waiting for our turns, as he was standing two people in front of me. Once I got up to order, I selected an herbal tea. We grabbed our cups and sat at a table across from each other.

I'd brought a bag with a journal and a book, and he did, too. We still had similarities about us: our love of reading and processing our inner thoughts. Within mine used to be prayers to a god I discovered was me. Over the years, my journaling became processing feelings and wishes for the life I longed to live.

Our conversation began with how we were both doing. Micah, rubbing his naked chin and mustache lips, asked how Moon was. I laughed and smiled; Micah didn't know Moon at all. Although Micah hadn't really met him yet, there had been a brief encounter between them at the park when Olea met his daughters shortly before we officially separated. We briefly talked about Olea and how amazing of a kid she was. How she's taken the divorce transition well. Then, Micah came out with what he was feeling—the words I'd always wished he would say to me one day.

"I didn't realize how much I relied on you to always make me happy." He stated matter-of-factly as his chin tilted down with his eyes looking up at me.

At that moment, I felt the heavens part with rain after a drought; witnessing the validation of the earth needing to be seen in all its excess heat. I finally knew what it meant to be seen by the clouds dancing above. I didn't need his rainy validation, but it felt just as good on my already moistened soil.

We never saw each other, which left us blind to never knowing ourselves. We were too busy trying to please and soothe the aches of our fragmented hearts.

Entering this conversation, I entertained the notion that Micah might ask me to return to fill the void in his aching heart. Thankfully, he didn't. And I confirmed the impossibility of it by replying to his question about how Moon was with an overflow of excitement, much like a waterfall cascading over rocks, joyously recounting the twists and turns of Moon and I's beautiful journey. This marvelous tale had become my life without Micah.

Yet, my soul remained tormented. That morning, I had awakened before the sun, an uncharacteristic occurrence. Internal battles raged within me. All the truths I had held back for the past twenty hours were finally set free.

As abruptly as it had begun, our conversation ended; leaving an eerie emptiness in its wake. Nothing was left to discuss after twelve years of cohabitation and mutual reliance. Our chaos of needing to soothe each other's lacks kept us together. And now, we had to face those alone. There was nothing more to share. I said goodbye and returned to my sacred dwelling on the mountainside.

Then, as if bravery hadn't asked enough of me throughout my entire life, my mom had also requested to talk that same day. I felt in deep alignment that afternoon, syncing up with the wise woman of me; who traipsed in the park, discovering that I needed to share with passion, to be a voice of truth. I laid in this vortex I've found in the trees near my apartment. Two trees curved up in a circle together with one jutting out, bent precisely for you to lay on; just to gaze into the vortex of the O shape the other trees had bent perfectly to make. I contemplated that maybe heaven touches earth here, yet life feels more like a continuation than this place where we'll find peace—realizing that peace can only be found through a well of endless adoration for oneself and all that is.

Toward the end of our phone call, my mother shared her belief that life is devoid of true happiness and that we can only cling to fleeting moments of joy. She placed her faith in an afterlife, where all wounds would be healed, juxtaposing it with the brokenness we endure in this present existence. My heart ached for her, carrying the weight of her lifelong grief.

Although I possessed fragments of her story, I knew it was fraught with pain as she tirelessly sought to mend others to find inner peace: a fallacy many of us struggle against. This delusion that peace lies external to ourselves; we aim to control the world around us to feel secure, yet true safety is only ever within.

In a month, we will reunite after two years of separation. During our video chat, I sat in bed, cocooned in blankets, as raindrops trickled down the windowpane. "Can Dad come?" she asked.

My response came with a firm, ease-filled "No."

"But what if he just stays with me and sees Olea?" She persisted by doing what she has always done: testing my boundaries; attempting to dismantle the walls I have erected, asking me to move them, just like she tries to make her heaven touch the earth while telling others to believe that if they just pray hard enough everything will feel okay.

Towards the beginning of my illnesses, when I was living in Denver with Olea at the age of three, I was wheelchair-bound and unable to do many things without hanging onto walls, afraid I would pass out at any second. My mom was visiting town, but off shopping with Sara, as Olea and I were home alone while Micah was at work. Suddenly, I didn't feel well and needed help. Laying on my gray rug on my living room floor, I had been doing gentle restorative yoga as Olea played with her baby dolls in the corner. Fearful I could not even get up again to make Olea lunch or help her if she got hurt, I called, desperate for her to come take Olea.

"Hello dear," my mom answered as the loud sounds of a mall scrambled in the background.

"Mom, can you please come to help me with Olea? I don't feel well. I'm terrified."

Instead of replying, "I'll be there as soon as possible." She said, "Just pray to God to make it better. I'm shopping right now with Sara."

Immediately, I hung up the phone and wept on my yoga mat. The tears surfaced, unable to be absorbed, like the reality of my illnesses by my mother who looked at my body, which seemed entirely and wholly able. Yet again, she refused to be the mother I needed. I crawled to the couch and turned on music for Olea to not worry why, yet again, Mommy could not have it together.

Somehow, I managed to get Olea and I through the next few hours with us living on the couch, asking her to grab snacks herself. A few hours later, my mom showed up with Sara right as Micah got home and began to take care of us.

I felt so furious with her. After she played with Olea for a minute, I asked her to leave.

Back on the phone call with my mom, in my Portland apartment, more healed, able-bodied, and living alone, I see this pattern of denying what's in plain sight to find the escape to soothe the hurt. I see the coping my mom's had to do and wish to rescue her. But as the silver hair caressed my neck, I remembered who I was. I no longer play the role of the rescuer. Instead, I float, and I radiate. That night, on that phone call, thousands of miles from her, I had to illuminate the lies she believed: that my dad wasn't safe. He hurt me. He stole me and other blood from this DNA we share.

Feeling fury rise to my voice, I breathed it out as I firmly replied, "No, Mom. Dad isn't safe. He hurt me very badly as a child…" I continued telling her some of what I knew, some of the memories, and how I had zero interest in having him in my life.

My mom walked outside their home, where my dad could no longer hear her conversation, and sat on one of her patio chairs. "What can I do?" was her only reply.

I wish she had wept. I wish I had wept. But we did what we've both been taught: to stand numb and state our feelings as if they weren't bubbling up in our throats instead of alien creatures outside us. Disassociation. I saw it in her glazed eyes and lips curled in, and in her throat tightening, asking how to fix it.

"Honor my boundaries. Respect my wishes. And do your work to become a safe person too."

The walls kept being asked to be rebuilt as she expressed her feelings, requesting me to hold her heavy bags while I refused to pick them up. I hung up the call with my mom, so proud of myself. I'd finally become her, this wise woman I had been striving to embody.

Both Micah and my mother had shown me the fragility of their own souls, demanding that I stitch them back together. I used to try to carry them all. Fix, just like her, yet I have no tool belt around my waist. I will not build either of them a silo holding all their baggage inside of my body. I've abandoned that construction and am instead saving my energy for myself.

I'm learning how to know I'm enough for myself. I cannot be enough for them, you, and my Moon. But I can create safety, honesty, and trust in my story and what I've been through. My path forward is self-discovery, where I uncover the depths of my soul and tread upon the sacred ground that I am destined to walk on.

After all those significant brave conversations, I curled myself into my bed, wrapped every blanket around me, nestled myself in my pillows, and celebrated the journey I'd come on. And in this unfolding journey, I know that I am not alone. The wise woman within me will continue to guide my steps, her silver hair shining as a beacon of truth and resilience. This is the new act. We've completely rewritten the script. It's no longer one we were reading, the one that has been given to us. Instead, it is one that is hand-crafted by every brave step I take.

SPEAKING IN WOBBLY STEPS

I picked up the phone, dialed the number listed. And listened to the dial tone until someone picked up.

A deep, male voice answered, "Rob isn't here." A bit confused, but knowing I was calling a bar, I ignored the statement and pressed on with my inquiry.

"Hi, is your open mic tonight just for musicians?"

"Not at all. We have comedians, poets, spoken word–it's great. We go until 2 a.m. So if you can't make it by 6:30 p.m. for sign-ups, we can still fit you in, maybe even for a second round. Come on down. It's a blast."

"Thank you so much." Hanging up, a surge of excitement washed over me. Tonight was the beginning, the first step towards fulfilling my intention for that May: to step onto the stage as often as possible, to share my stories, to be heard, and to stand unashamed. After spending most of my life being the quiet one, it was time to use my voice.

Growing up, I was afraid of my voice. As I auditioned for speaking roles in my high school theater, projecting was terrifying.

Every time I raised my voice to the pitch that allowed the whole audience to hear, it made me feel like I was screaming and yelling as if I was being attacked. Knowing what my body had been through in my childhood abuse, it's no surprise that this was my reaction to even my voice being loud. I'd always been one that had been constantly told to speak louder because I could not be heard. Micah used to get tired of asking me to speak up so often that when I'd talk and he couldn't hear me, he would get fed up with asking me to speak louder, so he just stopped listening. And I was tired of no longer being heard.

Before calling the open mic venue, I sifted through my writing for hours, searching for the piece that resonated. The venue was at a Southeast Portland bar. My most potent pieces were about being a mother and a woman. However, realizing these topics might not be the focus of my audience, I chose a story with a hint of whimsy that explored the concept of having to pretend to be strong to get your needs met— a narrative that more men could connect with.

I asked Moon if he'd join me. His response was simple. "Of course. Where else do I have to be?" We met there, arriving early. I secured the fifth spot, a number that had always followed me, from ID numbers to my phone number. This spot was enough to let the audience warm-up without enduring hours of anticipation.

Arriving at the bar, I was the first one to sign up. Others lingered, waiting for the paper to be set out, but I walked up and asked for it. At that moment, I wondered how often we wait for things to happen when all we need to do is take one step, say one word, and try one thing. This was the essence of how I wanted to live—to move forward towards my desires with the tenacity of a child learning to walk, reaching for what they wish, unafraid of the fall, eager to rise again and give it yet another go. I want this. I am this. And yet, I wonder why this fiery determination so often fades as we grow older.

Is failure so crippling that we forget how to stand back up? Or is it that in our infancy, we usually have a helping hand reaching out? Can we not extend that hand to each other as well? I see you trying.

I see you reaching. I see you. Let me cheer you on, for you are worth standing back up. Every. Single. Time.

I briefly left the bar. It was dark inside, and I was the worst patron for them, being someone who medically could not drink. The sun had just come out. It had been days since I last saw her, a common occurrence living in the cloud-covered Pacific Northwest. So I meandered down the street, soaking her in. Then, I caught the eye of a man who was behaving erratically. I immediately felt the alarms go off in my head: a female alone. This was a disaster. I grabbed my keys between my knuckles and approached the bar where people sat on a patio. I was turned enough away to be aware of my surroundings but wished I knew more self-defense. He walked away, and soon, Moon appeared behind me; immediately feeling relieved I wasn't here alone tonight.

This is where so many conversations begin, women having to live in so much grief. I've always wanted to dress in more ways, express myself, and feel good. I've always felt freer with less clothing than layers weighing on me. But encounters like these leave me wanting to cover up every inch of my skin because I do not want to be seen by anyone's unwanted attention as a threat to be devoured. I do not have the energy or desire to rant and rave about how we teach men to behave this way, to objectify women. However, I will gladly say that in my everyday life when I lived alone, I rarely faced this from most men.

The inside of the small bar was adorned with neon signs, a slightly sticky floor, a TV playing sports, and most of the tables around the stage peppered with people of all ages from mid-twenties to seventies; singles, couples and small groups of friends—a microcosm of life. The bar didn't seem like a place with a particular bit. The chairs were ordinary bar chairs. The decor was average. The drinks seemed to be expected. This was a neighborhood stop.

Moon and I immersed ourselves in the opening acts. We sat down at the side of the stage, as I didn't want to be able to catch Moon's eye while I was up there. His grin would be my undoing.

Then, a single man sat beside us, clearly on the prowl. I felt his eyes on me, and the moment Moon got up to get a drink, I felt him begin to hoover closer as if given an extended opportunity, he would try something. I felt it and ignored him.

I never spent much time in bars as a single woman. I was married through most of my early drinking years before I got sick and was always with a group of friends. But in the few moments of this encounter, I wondered why so many women go to bars. I felt more like a piece of meat on display than I felt like a human to be seen as anything more than my flesh. I wonder if women suddenly stopped going to bars as a refusal because we know we deserve so much more. Some women may want that, too, just for the physical connection, to which I share no judgment.

A few musicians played, and the fourth performers were a duo playing folk music. It was the perfect setup for me.

The MC announced, "...And now, welcome to the stage, Lumalia with spoken word."

Everyone clapped as I stepped onto the stage. I began to feel my palm sweat as I reached the platform on the side of the bar facing most of the booths of people before me, with Moon on my right.

As I grasped the microphone, memories of Micah's advice flooded in: how to project my voice to be heard. In our decade together, he'd been a musician; then later running a podcast, having me on as a guest once came to mind as another instance of learning to speak louder.

I drew a deep breath. The stage lights bathed me, and I found my focus. A group of three caught my gaze. "Hello, I'm Lumalia," I introduced myself. "And I play with subconscious pyrotechnics. This is called Unlearning How to Ghost Myself."

Beginning to read, a sense of belonging enveloped me. Home had always felt elusive, but on that stage, a harmony of ease and jitters surrounded me. My hand trembled, clutching the paper like a lifeline. This was my second time on stage reading my writing, my voice finding its feet like the wobble of an infant taking those first uncertain steps. Running with the excitement I felt, I let the passion roll out of me and slip off my lips like I had done this a thousand times before.

Suddenly, I noticed the clinking of glasses and the chatter of voices all fell quiet. The room hovered to an extinguished silence. Everyone was listening. I had their full attention. No one else on stage before me had quieted the room this much. This was my moment, and I was claiming it.

With each word, my excitement surged. My whole body lit up, and I read the rest of my story with as much passion as I knew how to do, with that much attention drawn toward me.

I caught the eye of one person in a booth; a young woman who saw straight into me. It felt like I was also reading her story, not mine.

"Mmhms" filled the room as an older gentleman in a booth alone nodded and took a deep breath, lifting his glass up to "cheers" my performance before he took a sip of his beer. My hands shook, and my armpits perspired. A mix of joy and fight-or-flight coursed through me.

Once I finished, the applause erupted—every last person in the audience cheered and whistled in a wave of affirmation. I did it! I finished saying thank you to everyone, bowed my head, and smiled bigger than I knew what to do with myself. My heart swelled with so much peace and calm, despite my perspiring glands. I knew this was where I was meant to be: using my voice and finally being heard for the first time in my life. I stepped off the stage, and was enveloped in Moon's embrace.

Returning home, I twirled in my apartment, a dance that whisked me back to my three-year-old self in my grandma Julia's kitchen. That same yearning for the spotlight to captivate attention refreshed my spirit.

My speech wasn't perfect or polished. Rushed, yes. Dramatic pauses were scarce. But it was a beginning, a profound first step towards reclaiming my voice, embracing a new me that had been beckoning since the age of three. Like an infant learning to walk, I took those initial, unsteady strides toward using my voice to reach out for precisely what I wanted.

SIZZLING SURPRISES

Growth inside me surged like a pot of boiling macaroni. Its energy rises out of its depths. Defying gravity, the water spills over to the edges. It burns and sizzles. And as it does, it makes room for the expansion and heating with all its attention. While feeling like this pot of macaroni on the edge of so much growth, I experienced the same sensation as the bubbles of delight surged. The hiss over the edge occurred—like something burning off, creating expansion within. Growing takes some burning around the edges when you go so fast.

In this state of rapid growth, I embrace a new relationship, healing from chronic illnesses, and daily shifts in lifestyle. I've found my point of not floating away like the hot air escapes the popped bubbles; I must ground in nature.

Stepping out of my usual boiling point, I went to a local rose garden. It's the beginning of the rose season. Blooms are unfurling from their deep sweaters. The sun shines stronger and warmer. We all begin to unravel from winter's tight, cloudy hug.

I strolled through the gardens and noticed different blooms peppering the roses, scattering polka-dot colors across the landscape. It felt almost as if you were sticking your hand into a bag of M&Ms, knowing each would be slightly different but just as delicious. With such radiance beckoning, it's impossible not to nuzzle your nose next to the bees inside the nectar of these glorious beauties, breathing in deep and letting the fragrances flood your entire nervous system. You become different, inhaling their radiance as you step in so intimately.

As I nestled my nose into every blossom I could get close to, I realized that roses only smell the first time. The second time my brain began to recognize its smell. It became duller. So, I began to pause between each rose. Letting my nose calibrate and try to get the first hit of the first rose I sniffed. But nothing felt as strong as her—that first blossom at the beginning of the rose garden's path.

Throughout my studies on healing, meditation, and flow states, I discovered the brain's remarkable ability to adapt to change and forget—a gift that often goes unnoticed. It fascinates me how we adapt, adjust, and get used to the surprise of change through all our senses.

It's been an exciting discovery for me to learn the power of surprise. However, it can cause Post-Traumatic Stress Disorder (PTSD) when sudden, traumatic events overwhelm our bodies and minds. One person may brush off a car accident and continue with their life. At the same time, another may develop extreme PTSD, constantly having fear when driving again.

Conversely, research reveals that surprise in the form of wonder and awe, such as gazing upon breathtaking vistas or experiencing the wonders of nature, can aid in the healing process for PTSD survivors.[1] Surprise seems to be the tie. One can heal and destroy in different settings, yet we can quickly become numb to its effects.

I draw parallels between the fleeting scent of roses and the familiar experiences we take for granted because it, too, has become common. Growing up in the Rocky Mountains, I was surrounded by majestic ranges with sweeping mountains at my feet. I traveled on many family vacations to more mountains, stunning vistas, and ranges that take their visitors' breath away. We'd go hiking, exploring, and skiing through these mountains that made you remember your smallness, while also providing a getaway to grand adventures. I failed to appreciate their grandeur as a child because they were my everyday backdrop, my familiar home.

Leaving for a small-town college in the middle of nowhere Tennessee, I encountered stark contrasts. Days of relentless rain became a new experience and an adventure to embrace. While others sought shelter, I stood outside, arms wide, letting the rain kiss me to no end.

The first time it rained for days straight, I remember standing out in my brand new colorful rainboots and red coat that made me feel like Carmen Sandiego, ready to conquer any adventure. The rain would come for days, dripping down every surface it touched; down our shoulders, down our umbrellas we would grab when it wouldn't give up. Everyone covered their heads and complained it wouldn't end. Yet, I'd find myself dancing in it for hours.

My classmates found my love for rain endearing but couldn't comprehend the water scarcity in the high desert where I grew up. Explaining how we had to water our grass to keep it green opened their eyes to a different perspective. While watering grass was novel to them, the drops of rain felt like liquid gold slipping down my throat.

The differences, I found, between the West Coast and the Deep South extended beyond weather. I realized the depth of racism when I heard my college classmates casually discuss disowning family members who would bring home someone of a different race. It shattered my innocence, and I couldn't fathom how skin color could alter someone's perception of another human being.

Unable to bear the cultural differences and abhorrent worldviews, I left the college after six months. I thought I was saying goodbye to the desert life I had grown up in, but upon my return, I drove to the foothills, laid my hands in the dirt, and kissed the feet of the glorious mountains.

I had missed my "watermelon mountains" more than ever. It took losing them, forgetting their magnificence amid the sea of my Tennessee dreams, to recognize the depth of my mountain girl identity.

I've lost a lot in my life already, not nearly as much as some. But becoming disabled was a lot for a new mother in her mid-twenties. When Olea was just three, and my illnesses progressed to the point where I couldn't walk more than a hundred feet without dizziness and fainting, I received a handicap sign to continue getting groceries. Having to ask for support at the grocery store at twenty-eight was extremely humbling. Years later, being able to walk holds the dearest place in my heart.

It makes me wonder what it takes not to forget the scent of a rose so quickly. Must we lose it and be surprised each time we receive fresh experiences? Ultimately, it permits us to live a life full of surprises. Letting things be novel or labeled as "the best ever" without feeling like it's silly to categorize everything as the best, even though we have many of them.

Discover new daily delights that dance around our senses, preventing us from growing too accustomed to the fragrance of a rose or the excitement of a pot of macaroni sizzling on the stove. Let it all sizzle, dazzle, and electrify us, for what an extraordinary life awaits when we discover daily wonder, even in the simplest moments—like boiling water in our kitchen.

---

1. Florence Williams, "The Nature Fix: Why Nature Makes Us Healthier, Happier, and More Creative," pg 255

FORGOTTEN BLOOD TIES

After not seeing each other for over three years (even though we lived in the same city in our adult life for a decade), my sister Sara, surprised me by wanting to send Olea a globe for Christmas; a thoughtful gift for her to track the places she'd been and dream of going in future travels.

Growing up, our family traveled often. Mostly boarding cruise ships, where my sister and I were placed in separate child care due to our four-year age difference. Still, sometimes, we'd take excursions with my family, where we would scuba dive with sea turtles and ride ATVs around Mayan forests drenched in mud. We'd gather over meals, where I remember sitting mostly quiet. At the same time, my parents talked, as I enjoyed charming the waiters to bring me sugar for my strawberries.

When Sara and I were home, we'd play travel together in my mom's bedroom. We packed our suitcases full of clothes and used my mom's room as the hotel and the master bathroom's garden tub as the airplane.

Yet, as we grew older, Sara mostly hung out with her friends. I'd tag along, alluring each of them to adore me; while Sara got annoyed at having to constantly hang out with her little sister. In contrast, her friends would say, "Oh, but she's so cute!" I'd add in my signature "pretty eyes," then I'd convince her and her friends to push me in a red convertible go-cart as the battery frequently died, crying to my mother if she did not.

You'd often find Sara in her bathroom, spending hours getting ready and taking care of her golden rapunzel-like hair so thick it could only hold one loop of a hair tie around it. Sara had luscious, wavy hair. While growing up, I had thin, fragile hair that rarely held a curl no matter how much hair product my mom used. She'd spend hours straightening her hair while I secretly wished she kept it in the stunning, wild waves it held. I hoped one day my hair would be as full as hers.

I always wanted her full attention, so I'd frequently barge into her bathroom door with my boom box playing Hilary Duff's CD on repeat; singing to her, "You're so yesterday!" We'd giggle, and I'd sit on the countertop watching her do her makeup. Eventually, she'd kick me out so she could meet her friends, and I'd return to my bedroom, singing, dancing, and pretending to be a choreographer.

As we spoke on the phone that cloudy Saturday morning, Olea was with Micah for the weekend. I was caught off guard by a rush of emotions. Tears raced down my cheeks like a fast-moving current. This sister I had always felt so distant from, had gone out of her way to think of her niece and wanted to make something special for her.

This sister, with whom I had grown distant to, due to the scars of our shared childhood wounds, reached out with tenderness and love. My sister and I's connection had been strained, marred by the weight of unspoken pain and the awareness that Micah knew more about me than she ever did. I had pushed her away, protecting myself from the past and perhaps denying us the chance to be true sisters.

We grew up traveling a lot, and even though we were never close,

I feel she loved me more than I ever knew how to love her. I was always surviving, trying not to poke the bear of anyone, and be happy—just like we were taught to do.

One of the most influential counselors I worked with, who understood the depths of my traumatic experiences, once told me there was a reason she and I were never close. Abusers separate children so that the one that is being abused doesn't snitch. For this reason, these tears flooded my face. A dam had been released, as I saw the beautiful person I've come to miss, my sister; who's always loved me so well, especially when I didn't know how to be with her. She's always been a phone call away.

Especially that particular day in my mid-twenties, I fell on the kitchen floor. It was the beginning of my Dysautonomia when I started passing out, and I was too sick to walk. She was the one who made me promise to go see a doctor and find out what was wrong with me. She was the one who put in a word for me to see the top cardiologist in our city so that I could get the help I needed.

Yet, I pushed her away. Micah knew the toxicity in my family and encouraged me to take space for myself. And I did need the space. But I mourn for us and the sisterhood we didn't have, the one she always tried to pursue but I always pulled away from. I never shared much with her. But today, I called her. After divorcing Micah, I'd met Moon and wanted to tell her before my mom inevitably would, so she wouldn't feel sad about not hearing it from me.

I missed not having a sister, and while I don't know what can be mended or what relationship we can have, I'm filled with a mixed rage for the one who stole this from us and this bond we were supposed to have. I see not only my dad who took it away but also how I let Micah be my voice too often.

Moon has been instrumental in my healing journey. He sees the best in people, yet his presence has helped me stand solid in my boundaries and protect my energy. In my best attempt to not trauma bond with Moon, I became hyper-aware of not being responsible for his emotions or mine, while also learning solid boundaries. Through our relationship, I've learned the value of setting boundaries and not feeling responsible for emotionally regulating others' feelings or experiences. Moon's unwavering support has allowed me to find safety in vulnerability and embrace the power of saying "no" when needed.

This beautiful new space with Moon has reminded me that I get to decide who gets to be in my life and that family isn't privileged to me just because we share blood ties. I've discovered the empowerment of setting boundaries and choosing the relationships that nourish my soul. As the rain continues to fall, it feels like the earth is releasing its wounds with each season, just as I am releasing the men who took away what was rightfully mine: the bond of sisterhood. The abusers who stole my innocence and silenced my voice will no longer define me.

I pick up the shattered pieces of my reality and claim them as my own. I am intentional, no longer lost. This journey is not easy, and I don't know what the future holds for my relationship with my sister and family. I don't have to be estranged from my sister, and I especially don't have to be estranged from myself, who got stolen away by the abuse of generations accumulating in the snow.

The darkest layer is now brown and worn down as I come in with my four-wheel snowplow, making the roads clear again. This time, I may walk down a new one, just like I've always done. Yet this time, I'm not lost. I'm intentionally leaning into my gut, trusting everything is beautiful if you know how to look.

SAND IN OUR EYES

We stood at the edge of the cliff, nothing but the Pacific Ocean ahead of us with sand in our eyes and exasperated lungs from all we'd been holding.

Earlier that morning, Olea, Lindsay, and I gathered ourselves in white dresses, beginning our day of adventures by chasing a waterfall in the valley, just south of Hilo, on the American-stolen paradise land of Hawaii. My close friend Lindsay, with the ends of her hair bleached, and a petite frame, radiated a kindness and brightness for life that followed her everywhere she went. She came with us to celebrate my new little family, just Olea and I, after the divorce. This trip was for us to celebrate a new chapter and for me to promise Olea, despite all the changes, I was still her mama. I was going to do what so few mothers get to do: hold a sacred ceremony vowing my commitment to us both, that we'd live only a beautiful life from here on out.

As we reached the waterfall, we were surprised by how far away and gated off the cascading beauty of crystal syrup rushing down was. This felt disappointing. The view was divine, but nothing quite like the presence we regularly feel standing behind the surge of wind that catches your breath. Where we live in Oregon, it is waterfall land. Hundreds of waterfalls litter the mountains. You can get so close to some of them that they could become the most powerful shower you've ever stepped into. But, this tourist spot in Hawaii was far from our "normal" waterfall adventure experiences; with its gates, guards standing by to ensure tickets were paid, and paved trails. Wonder slipped past me, and I tried to cling on as I asked myself, "Where are you, beloved Awe?"

The anticlimactic waterfall hike set the tone for the day, truly beginning with how I wholly ignored many parts of me. I want to feel more than how many more steps until the end. I was stuck in the loop of finishing instead of enjoying the journey—oh, how many of us get stuck in that same circle?

Fatigued and exhausted, I wanted to linger in bed for hours that day. Yet, being on the Island for six short days in a winter loop around the sun, I felt the rush to squeeze it all in. "Get in every last drop because we won't have this again." Scarcity.

I'm a recovering addict learning what the slow sips of warm soup in your bowl means, instead of slugging it down in delight; finding it just burning your tongue. Yet, I lived fresh inside her, thinking I had to push past everything my body was calling for because we had to go today to experience this adventure.

Halfway through our Hawaiian waterfall hike, Olea proclaimed boredom amidst this wild jungle, to which I suggested, as all mothers do, "Boredom is only an opportunity to find something good." She tried her best and quickly found five interesting things but continued in the childhood song of being tired and just as exhausted as I was.

Lindsay was with us and entirely in her own zone, stroking her black box with its shutter, clicking and capturing the delights that dazzled her eye. She was a beautiful balance between Olea and I, who were mostly exhausted and cranky. Despite our fatigue, we continued toward a highly recommended Green Sand Beach for two more hours.

This gorgeous beach called to me, as emerald green appeared in a meditation a few months before and often after the divorce. Its presence reminded me that I'm abundant and can experience a love that doesn't give itself away. Everywhere I went, I kept discovering the color green, reminding me to keep drawing myself closer to a life outside of the bondages of codependency, which I'd spent a lifetime in. I realized that I no longer needed to subscribe to the self-sacrificial narrative that I'd been thrust into from a young age; particularly during my Christian marriage, where I always tried to earn someone else's love. What I truly needed was to love myself. Now, with my daughter by my side, I had the opportunity to rewrite this narrative for us both.

When researching our trip, Janet, a fellow mom from Olea's school who had once lived on the big island, shared with me, "You need to check out Beach Number Five, the volcano and Green Sand Beach. Let me pull up a map and show you."

I grabbed my phone and pulled up the locations she told me about. She pointed her finger at the map and said, "Green Sand Beach is really neat. It's at the edge of the island but is really beautiful."

The significance of this color took on a life of its own, fitting seamlessly into our plans. It was almost surreal to think that such a place existed, unlike the usual brown or black sand typically associated with the Hawaiin island's volcanic origins. Here, the sand was a breathtaking green.

As we delved into learning about Hawaii before our trip, Olea and I discovered that the green sand at this beach owed its color to a mineral called Olivine. What struck us with more fascination was that the letters "Ol" were nestled within Olivine. And with a peculiar step even further, we then learned the Hawaiian name for this beach is Papakōlea, which held her full name. It felt like destiny had guided us to this place that held a piece of her name in its very essence. We were meant to go there.

As we planned to have a ceremony on this beach, I vowed to never repeat those mistakes again, and to help Olea see the innate value she has, too. Mother Nature was on our side to help us remember these divine truths.

After leaving the waterfall, we drove a few more hours to reach the main road that led us to Papakōlea, the Green Sand Beach parking lot. The scenery had drastically changed from luscious tropical forests, to a petroglyph volcano, to sweeps of grass met with blue skies and the ocean cliff just a few sniffs away. We all noted this felt more like Ireland than the southern tip of this tropical island. Animals ran wild, greeted by new babes with moos and nays. We all delighted in the magic of experiencing so many drastic views in just a few hours of dashed lines and vanishing views.

The rustic parking lot of Papakōlea was nothing more than spray-painted red dirt and cars piled up. Locals greeted us, asking if we needed a ride. Then, a middle to late-aged couple showed up with their hiking poles. I thought to myself, as I graciously declined offers from all the locals, "If they're up for this, we can too." I wanted the long route to take in every breath of the view, reclaim my wonder, and remember the sacredness of this day. "I'm choosing to be lavished upon today, this day of promising me back to myself and committing to my daughter to embody self-love."

Determined to walk, we packed our bags. Lindsay sweetly carried one of ours to help me keep more energy, forever questioning if my illnesses would flare today. We set out on the route.

Initially, we followed a trail that appeared like deep water channels carving into the red sand, forming miniature canyons. These canyons were topped with small patches of grass, giving them an enchanting appearance. As we ventured deeper into these mini canyons, it became evident why only locals dared to drive on these roads. The route was intricate, resembling a jigsaw puzzle shaped by the relentless forces of rain.

We made it a quarter of the way, and with each view was a sight to pause and sigh at, asking ourselves, "Is this really my life?"

The visual eye-candy danced before me; teal-white water mixed and crashed, splashing against the cocoa black-holed rocks, and grass waving in the wind like the caterpillar crawling to no end. I was whirled into magic. However, my sweet Olea stood at my feet, overwhelmed with sand in her eyes, exhaustion in her toes, and a belly longing for food. She so sweetly only had a few complaints, and in my own motherhood weariness, I had only short words to comfort her. I desperately wanted this experience to be magical for her, too. But yet again, I pushed us both past our limits, asking too much of us.

This has been our life. I have so little left for her when I've pushed too far, like a fire burned out with only embers to keep us warm. We want to live our lives, but both dance in the Aries sun—bound to burn each other out. We're still learning to replace the water that Micah's spirit held for us both, dousing us out when we'd gone too far. He'd often ask to be done on the adventures. Yet, his story here was no longer a part of us, which was precisely why we were here in the royal green sand—to remember our divinity, our promises to be whole without him.

Later on our trip, as we went to have a lazy day on a beach, Olea asked me, "Can we bring Daddy back here one day to show him around? He could even stay in a separate home."

"That would be very sweet. Do you miss Daddy?" Imagining this had to be so hard for her, to be without him after her whole life was experienced with the three of us together.

"Kinda." She replied as if she didn't want to hurt my feelings that she, too, felt a little like the black-holed volcanic rocks, as a piece of her was missing while embracing all the splashes of life.

We left the subject there to burn in the air. It had only been six months since we separated.

I'd finally come to my end. It had been two years in the making, but I'd finally gotten the sense of self-worth and power to trust that I deserved to be loved and cherished in a way Micah wasn't capable of. It took me two years of potent people encouraging me that I deserved to be happy, too.

At my end, terrified of damaging Olea, I asked for a powerful sign to leave him. The next night, I had a dream where my friend Apatha, having known so much suffering herself, led me with her gentle guidance and walked me into a doctor's office for a heavy appointment. She sat next to me as the doctor told me I had breast cancer, and they weren't sure how well I'd respond to treatment or survive.

I woke up finally brave enough. I walked out to Micah sitting on our outdoor patio swing, while Olea was off playing with the dogs in the yard far away, "I want a divorce."

He didn't argue at all. He just nodded his head and sat silently for at least an hour until I met him in the kitchen later.

Olea was only seven. In meditation, I asked for a vision to help her understand what was happening. Immediately, I was given this vision I shared with her after sharing it with Micah.

We sat in our shared office on a soft red carpet. I started with, "There were once two caterpillars, and they loved each other very much. And they tried to fit into one chrysalis. Then, they had a baby caterpillar named Olea. But because all three were in one chrysalis, no one could grow to become a butterfly. So we had to go find our own chrysalises." She nodded in understanding as I continued to explain how we would be separating into two different homes so we could all go and become butterflies.

She never once was upset about our separation because she knew deep down this was better for all of us. Too often, Micah and I would spend many days deep in grief, trying to dig ourselves out of the ache we felt in our marriage. The loneliness I experienced, and the freedom Micah so deeply craved, pushed and pulled us so often. She may not have understood, but the shift in me opened me up to have more capacity to love her in ways because I'd been too busy trying to love Micah.

Along our hike, at the edge of the Big Island, we continued noting the majestic views. Yet, I got into the space again where my body screamed louder than my luster for landscape candy, sticky and sweet. But this time I had unwrapped too much. My legs ached, and my body wondered how much it would cost me to be present tomorrow. I wondered why I said yes to hiking instead of the local ride. I wanted to prove I could do this. "I'm well. I've traveled halfway across the pacific to be here, just us girls. We don't need your "man's" help to carry our bags. And, oh no. I especially don't want your collection of sea shells with your shame scratched in them." I had lugged that for twelve years and wanted to leave it here; right here on the island where Mama Earth burns out new flesh and destroys, turning ash into a cooling, luscious land where anything can grow.

Except, I think I destroyed too much that day. My body made the sacrifice again of what I thought I wanted. Yet again, I over-exhausted myself.

Our tired legs led us to pause and wait for Lindsay. She had wandered into her own world, thankfully unencumbered by our achy moods. We waited for her, and suddenly, out of seemingly nowhere, the last truck of the day drove up. The driver, Alfred, waved at us, "Do you want a ride?"

I nodded to try to shout against the wind, "Yes! Thank you!"

Olea and I were both done walking despite the gorgeous views. And she was done with the endless wind with her aching belly that half of a Larabar could barely fill.

We hopped into Alfred's truck. The bed was full of an Indian family packed in like ants, delighted to be together inside a honey pot, all purely delighted and giggling as they joggled in the bed. We climbed into the cab and we relaxed with the ease of air conditioning and no sand blowing in our hair.

I sighed, feeling seen and held at a time when I had forgotten to cradle myself. I am thankful that when at my end, heaven would bring people like Alfred along to give us rides.

I wondered how long I'd continue to neglect myself for, for the sake of something beautiful, or how long this war would wage on;

keeping me from feeling well in any vertical posturing as I still battled lingering symptoms of Dysautonomia. But, I let myself find ease
in how we're always held by angels we usually call strangers.

Alfred told us stories of this land, how the rocks gathered in the
distance were not just random but foundations of the native Polyne-
sians. We were in awe, while part of me wished my feet still touched
the ground so I could feel those walls, know their stories, and hear
their hearts. But the wheels found the hills to get us up and out as we
chased the quickly departing brief winter sunlight.

Once we finally arrived, we had forty minutes left after our hour-
long hike and truck ride. The cliffs were golden, and the cove light
was almost gone. At the top of the cliff, I decided to share my vows
with Olea.

The wind nearly blew her over as I set up a video. Meanwhile,
Lindsay sweetly took pictures. Olea was so brave to stand with me
near the edge.

I gathered next to her in our matching white dresses. I looked into
her eyes and began proclaiming the story of just us now.

The one where it is her and I. Acknowledging the troubles of her
life: having a sick mommy, a struggling set of parents, and having to
pull her out of her community at age five, as we moved to Oregon.
She's been so courageous and strong for all she's endured. I proclaimed
the pride I had in her for her gentleness and bravery. And I promised
her the sacred things only a mother who has touched death can.

I'll forever keep our ceremony sacred, not just because of these
promises of how I would hold her, as a mommy without her daddy
sharing the same home with me, but because I got to share them
with her out loud. How many mothers get to have these promises put
into breath?

How many sacred ceremonies could we have with our beloved
children to often remind them of all the ways we're promising to
hold them? I find it frequent in between meals, car rides, bedtime
snuggles, and after disagreements. But what if we made it more

sacred for them to hear the promises of our love and commitment to keep learning how to better support them as they grow and change each year?

Despite the wind that threatened to knock us down and the exhaustion in every ruffle of our bones, I rejoiced in the fact that I got to proclaim these words to the dearest thing I get to hold on earth.

When I finished, she said she felt sad after our vows. I hugged her close. Tears held their place as we wrapped ourselves up and descended the steep hill to the cove where the sand caramelized emerald green.

We quickly slipped on our matching velvet green dresses and let Lindsay take photos of us prancing around the beach. Ah, what is this abundant life but one to be wholly devoured in giant bites— green dresses on the green sand on the southernmost coast.

The light flickered on the rocks as we climbed around some of the edges of the cliff. Then we splashed on the Olivine Green Sand Beach near the water for just a few moments before returning to Alfred's car, full of giggles and golden joys as the sun set.

I had envisioned a time to say my own vows to myself, too, at this time. But in the swiftness of pulling it all together, I hadn't made my vows or told them to myself. Regret could fill me, but I decided to make nothing of it and promised myself this would be about a rebirth of me, too. So, two nights later, I wrote them out.

My most meaningful vow was to not abandon myself. This was the scar of this divorce. I had always chosen Micah first. Hoping he could know love by the fierce love I wanted to show him. But as any story with this plot will go, it's impossible to help someone see the love they can only find by accepting their own blood weaving within their veins. Yet, I tried to enter into his veins, only to find after twelve years I mostly just got under his skin. His body filled up with his detest of me more than admiration or cherishing: the two I requested often and always found empty, despite my pleas and pursuit to heal the wounds we both so wretchedly caused each other.

After our explorations on the beach, we jumbled back into the truck through the dusk light, holding all the greatest delights in our hearts, sandy toes, and ocean-blown tangled hair. As we bobbed in the seats, we watched the evening sun illuminate the grass as it waved us goodnight.

At the beginning of this journey, I thought this ceremony would mostly be for me. Still, looking back, I now see it was mostly for my Olea; for her to know it would be powerful for us both to grow. We're not perfect. Sometimes, we push too hard but still find joy. It's been a gentle reminder that sacrifice has been so deeply written into me that it will take time to turn it from fresh lava, allowing the ocean to cool me and be turned to the Olivine green sand I now get to call my beloved daughter.

As the sun set, we said goodbye to these messages of sacrifice. We stepped into the nighttime darkness of the unknown, saying hello to the reminder that, yet again—abundance is our legacy, despite the sand in our eyes.

OPENING THE CLOSET OF GRIEF

The door is closed, the very door I had tirelessly worked to open again. Within this closet was a portal to the person I've always felt I was but only knew in small doses through the scent she seeps out beneath the seams.

I finally opened her after years. It took years of gentle coaxing and unwavering self-guidance, but I finally unleashed her. She held these pieces of me for decades, and once I cracked her open, out tumbled the sorrow, the playful, the joyful, and the stories of me fresh as the orange juice I squeezed through my juicer that morning.

Throughout my battles with illnesses, I was required to follow my body's wisdom to journey deeper into self-discovery. It's there that I found eating more plants, resting, living in harmony with nature, listening, and following my soul's calling to build something bigger than myself. I allowed myself to create safety, which I hadn't realized I was cultivating all along, simply by following the whispers.

Together, hand in hand with this closed piece of myself, we journeyed deep into the uncharted territories of my soul, uncovering depths I didn't know could exist within me. I listened to her, felt her fears, and slowly encouraged her to walk alongside me; growing wings to soar to new heights.

Yet, in my quest for wholeness, I kept pushing too far, letting my feelings of inadequacy define my worth in my effort to heal. I'd become the bully lurking behind my sweet smile. I've always had this side of me that can become insistent on overcoming every edge, refusing to heed requests for rest or caution. In these moments, it's as if the word "stop" becomes a challenge to push harder, become more innovative, and become better.

Endurance runners and athletes often push their limits but do so with connection and trust in their bodies. Even though they've never done this new task or new experience, they can work towards what hasn't been achieved with practice and accomplishment because they first hold faith in their ability to achieve the previously inconceivable, with the anchoring in themselves and the power of their imagination.

However, I didn't approach it the same way. I ignored safety roadblocks, disregarded the harnesses and crash pads that I had in place, and instead recklessly solo-climbed, insisting that I could conquer any obstacle—even if it meant sacrificing my well-being. With my stubbornness winning, I replied to her, "If you won't come, I can do this with or without you." And it's with that, my body revolted again.

She shouted with her rashes and infections exploding in me, "We've gone too far, yet again."

The consequence was evident as my body revolted once again. The door began to close, and with it, all the freedom, openness, creativity, and joy I had discovered through my journey now felt out of reach.

Grieving over the pain I've caused myself, I realized that my struggles go beyond just external influences; it's about self-abuse, replicating patterns of abuse within myself. No one else is to blame anymore; the responsibility lies with me, with my lack of listening and constant pushing.

I'll weep. I'll apologize. But I know the only thing that will allow this piece of me to feel safe again is to go gently this time, to continue to get better at listening and honoring, to take no as no, and to trust there is no rush despite any existential crisis metaphorically brewing. I've been sick before, my symptoms speaking louder than my voice so I'll lean in deeply again to listen. It's winter now and near the darker days of the year. The seasons even suggest I will be okay with being closed, too.

Yet, I miss and long for the days when I felt so free and open; when the truth would spill out of me like a leaky faucet insistent on being irreplaceable. I felt the most at home that I had ever felt with her open. But I must honor her here, in this season, closed. I must hold her tightly and apologize, listening to what she needs to just even be with me.

This is the ugliness, the utter tornados of childhood sexual abuse from our primary caretakers. Those of us who have faced such wretchedness have to relearn how to not abuse ourselves.

Many turn to self-destruction, feeling a sense of worthlessness to be alive. I've seen it in others dear to me. Yet this one, this form of my own self-destruction, feels so sneaky and clever. It is as if it could be disguised as hustle and efficiency; dare I even say, productivity, in a need to prove I'm enough as I glitter with my ability to heal.

It's time to surrender the masculine wound of not feeling enough, and extinguish the wildfire fueled by abuse, allowing a rebirth in the earth's womb where seeds break open and root. (Isn't it ironic that a baby's first attempt at finding food after birth is called rooting, too?)

Nature reminds me that healing takes time, that progress should be slow, and that rest is crucial. It's a reminder that we're worthy to take the long, scenic route home to find rest for this weary soul, ending the lifetime's worth of trauma and abuse etched into these bones.

From now on, I'll softly whisper to her each day, "I love you. This time, we'll journey together at your pace and on your terms." Safety was shattered again in my world, which has known so little.

So, for now, I'll sit here and let her weep, allowing myself to grieve all that's been done to us. I'll take responsibility for the patterns we're still replicating and promise never to repeat them again. No more rolling stops for us. We're choosing the long, scenic route home, where our weary souls can rest.

As we sit, taking in the view of the ocean, I promise to let go of the hold that's been driven by trauma and sing only songs of liberation and freedom. No longer propelled by trauma, it will be just us forever together. With my heart leading, I'll learn what it means to break free from replication and embrace the fullest expression of my being—only propagating a life of love and honoring every piece of me as a beautiful mosaic no longer tucked away in my closet of grief.

YOU ARE NOT YOUR STORIES

You are not your stories.
Your stories are a part of you.

They once held a piece.
Like a breath they flow,
in
and
out.

Honor each chapter,
each character,
each scene,
the memory of
dance and play.

Promise to never
let your stories explain
who you are.

TWO DIVIDED BY FOREVER

Anomaly: I should have split into two different personalities
with the amount of abuse I faced as a child,
or at least that is what my trauma therapist said.

I held myself together by sneaking Oreo cookies
from my aunt Margot's bottom cabinet
while she smiled at me,
knowing I didn't just have two in each hand
but one in my mouth
and five in my belly.
Knowing, herself, what it
meant to have to do anything to survive the oppression
of the men who promise to protect us by giving us life.

But I didn't.
I kept going with my sugar highs
and excuses to never be home, to leave the city

the moment I could get straight A's and pass my AP exams.
To run away, run far away,
and make myself something new.

I didn't let myself become two.
I allowed myself to forever become.
And I think that's why I didn't split in two
because I knew I didn't hold just one plus one.
I held infinity, unable to touch just one destiny.

So please don't limit yourself, or me,
as you try to identify with your stories
of who you were told you had to be,
or who you must become.
Because if my belly can be full of "just two cookies"
when it held eight,
then we can step into a loop
of a quantum realm,
instead of staying only in the stories
where the definition can limit.

Let's instead only give a depiction
to the perception of space between atoms,
that is mainly made of 99.9% nothingness.
We exist as space despite our delineation.
It's there I hold hope past the stories
of how I've been told how to be.
Primarily atoms, we're all mostly unknown,
daily becoming.
How would you exist
if you, too, rested in always being an anomaly?

SPITTING OUT CAKE

My DNA carries their imprints, a legacy of nurturing and life lessons. I am grateful for the beautiful truths they imparted on me: the importance of caring for one's belongings, diligent work, braiding hair, the ability to see all perspectives, and the capacity to love even when faced with ugliness. They taught me to stop and notice the flowers, recognize my own beauty, and never give up when I fall down. I could spend a lifetime crediting them for all the good they've done and the person they've helped me become.

However, there is one undeniable truth that I can no longer ignore: the safety they failed to teach me, the harm they caused, the emotional poison they fed me, and the lies I was told to keep.

It's time to tell my truth. To say what was declared to be kept quiet, about how mean dad was when things didn't go his way, about how I was touched, used, and manipulated to pleasure men before I knew what my body was, all under their aware eyes.

Now, I am committed to reestablishing a sense of safety within my own body, free from the burden of worrying about their well-being.

Throughout my childhood, I remember my mother always demanded that I apologize for hurting someone else's feelings, but I rebelled against that notion. I refused to take responsibility for how others felt when I didn't feel responsible for doing wrong to them. While a true piece of my emotional immaturity was a lack of empathy that eluded me, deep in me, I knew I could not hold someone else's emotions.

Under my parent's household, my life was never truly my own. My life felt like it was someone else's to use because of the abuse. My only true home, my body, was never just mine. So when asked to hold a person and their emotions, I hit my boiling point and refused empathy. It was my only way to separate myself from others, especially my parents and other abusers.

The closer I stayed to my parents, the more I realized we were still too connected. How easy it was to slip back into old roles that left me out of my self-autonomy and the same truth that they never truly saw me but wanted me to rescue them from their own experiences and absorb their emotions.

During the early days of the pandemic, Micah, Olea, and I drove eight hours from Denver to where they lived in the desert. We wanted to say goodbye to them, along with some old friends, before we moved across the country to Oregon. My parents were just getting over COVID-19, and I was content not to stay with them like we used to before my memories returned. So we stayed with Micah's friend and met my parents for one day with masks at a park.

We drove up to a nearby park on that sweltering day in August. And lathered ourselves in sunscreen and hats to keep from burning as the sun beat ceaselessly. Grabbing our water bottles from the car, Olea ran with Micah to the playground. She was only six, so he went to help her reach different features, including a zipline at the play structure. Still in the middle of chronic fatigue, I found some shade on the edge to sit. Concrete met the bark in the play area, a stark contrast between something solid and something that gives in as you jump on it. I wanted to become more like the concrete with my family.

Per usual, my parents arrived fifteen minutes late with their masks on. I let them hug Olea but was afraid that they were contagious to get too close to them. It was as if this illness was perfectly timed to divinely protect me from having to absorb any more of them after decades of being forced to.

We sat and spoke for a few moments. My mom played with Olea and then told me about all her church friends and what they were up to.

"Do you remember Kathy?" I'd shake my head "no," as I often had forgotten about the people she knew.

"Well, her and her daughter just went to San Jose and had a lovely time. They told me how they saw whales and sharks, but then they got sick flying back home. Oh, and Michelle, she's having a hard time being divorced and lonely. We go to the movies weekly."

Never once did she share anything about her life. Her ability to deflect and never actually confront her emotions or experiences is astounding. But it also made her unable to listen to me in ways that pushed me further away from them.

The shadows began to grow longer, and our bellies were hungry. I tried to talk to my dad while my mom played with Olea. "How are you doing?"

Gazing off at Olea, he spoke to me as he sat on the bench. Both our bodies were burdened with too much generational trauma, and had slowed us down from the fierce people we both are.

"I hope you all don't get this. It's horrible. I wasn't sure I was going to make it. Good thing you're young and healthy. It's been beating us old people up," he said, never quite making eye contact with me.

A rock hit my stomach. For the past two years, I'd been bedridden, disabled, and unable to work and care for Olea. My dad knew this, yet completely ignored it.

I was done. Done not being seen by my parents. Done not being supported. Done not telling the truth.

I got up, walked over to Micah and said, "I need to go."

After that, it only took two years of minimal contact with them to realize how much my body yearned for deep space from them; to not have phone calls pretending everything was ok, or not having to send pictures, unsure what my dad would do with them. However, it wasn't an easy decision to come to.

Wrestling with the yearning to bid them farewell, I desired to give my body the space and respite to discover what life can be like without constantly catering to their passive requests. They were never big, but repeatedly invalidated my reality that I was actively trying to heal. I could no longer exist in a place where this little girl who was so hurt was ever told she cannot be real.

They are fully alive but I asked my mind to exist as if they were gone, wishing for their death from me. Yet, how does one say such goodbyes?

Just a year before, we had bid farewell to Micah's mother. It was a relatively easy decision. Her volatile nature, the constant slicing with her words, and the perpetual harm she caused our family made it clear that she was toxic. Supporting Micah's desire to remove her from our lives made sense.

Superficially, my parents strived to connect, asking about our well-being and requesting pictures, phone calls, visits, and trips together. They would comply with any request that seemed apparent. Still, they never fulfilled the one that required them to acknowledge the harm they inflicted, a "sacred" secret so deeply repressed within them, buried beneath layers of indulgence. I, too, could indulge and drown my emotions in the illusion of metaphorical pleasure-inducing "cake," becoming a character akin to Wall-E, massive and immobile, except to seesaw.

However, I refused to bury my emotions by pretending everything was okay. Instead, I channeled every ounce of pain into shattering the generational patterns that dictate, "This is how it must be."

I wanted to shout to them, "Go ahead and force-feed your cake to someone else because I will keep my mouth closed until my heart bursts with its own truth, sharing my story exactly as I wish."

In this paradoxical state, I sat on the scale, weighing the heaviness of putting what was still alive within me to rest.

After moving across the country to Oregon and towards the second year of the pandemic, my soul demanded that I fully reclaim all of my life. The toxic dynamics of my relationship with Micah imprisoned me. I deserved happiness, adoration, and profound love—qualities he could not provide. We sought solace in each other, he the victim and I the rescuer, trying to heal the wounds inflicted by our parents. But resentment became our melody, the chorus of our soap opera, always on the verge of ending.

Then, one day, I allowed myself to dream of a different life, of a man who could truly meet my needs. I listed the attributes I loved about every person I'd ever met, photographed, befriended, and adored. My friend Ben's bigness in a room to make everyone laugh, my old neighbor Trevor's kindness in loving every baked good I made to share, the utter bliss of every man I photographed as he looked at his bride, the passion of the couple who loved to run and skip together just for giggles, the artist curiosities of Micah, the men online who took photographs of the world they traveled, the painter with his fingers filthed from falling in love with the female form, the love of kids in my friend Daniel, the ability to stand up and fight for me when I was wronged (my friends Daniel and Ben did this after our church said I couldn't host yoga classes anymore), the tenderness of the doctor who looked me in the eye and said I believe your illness is real, the adoration of my grandmother Julia, as she smiled every time I performed for her in her kitchen, hallway, or living room, playing the piano, my family's love of sports, the need to tell stories of my mother, the praise of my grandfather Bill, as he took us around to every coworker when we visited him at the Military base grocery store Commisary while he bagged groceries late into his seventies. And as if he had been waiting his whole life miraculously, my beloved Moon, embodying these exact traits, appeared in my reality mere weeks later.

But before I met Moon, I had one final request. I asked Micah, "Will you become him? Will you step into the role of this man, this relationship that I desire alongside me? Will you live this life with me?"

His reply was, "As friends, that sounds nice."

I yearned to be consumed, adored, and enveloped in another person's skin. I knew I had to bid him farewell at that moment, too.

And so Moon, the love of my life and now partner, entered my life, quite literally.

I have experienced this death before but I had an open door and a vision to guide me this last time.

Having to say goodbye to my parents now felt like an open door leading into unknown shadows. Perhaps this is where I must begin my grieving, for it is through grieving that I will find the freedom to let go.

Who can I become when the lies I was told to keep are brought into the light? Where will I go when I envision a life imbued with true masculine love, protection, and care?

I told my mom this truth and promised myself I'd create the life I desired. I set the boundaries, drew the lines, and told her I needed space. It was her turn to do her own work of not hiding from the past, but my future required I go forward without her and my dad's ties.

Moon and my closest friend came to support me in my decision fully. They came to help me in the transition as I severed the identity of being 'their' child, into finally being completely my own person.

I still wrestle with the coding by which we are connected, my parents and I. But now, it's from a deeper distance that allows me in each moment to set aside being quiet and finally letting my truth and my voice be heard, especially as I claim my body back, along with my right to say "no."

RUNNING LOPSIDED

Each day is new but also the same, as am I. Some days feel slow, and some days long. Some days fast, and some days quick. At this moment, I feel distanced from everything. Neither grounded nor soaring, but caught in between. Honestly, it's a sensation akin to drowning, lost in a sea without a discernible up or down.

The shadows of reality have finally caught up with me. It's just me facing the vast expanse ahead. Space and financial security seem distant, appearing momentarily before slipping away like elusive dreams. This is the rhythm of running a business, of charting my own course. I reach for my desires, hoping the next venture and the next investment of time and energy will bring me closer to my aspirations. My lost slipper is gone, and I thought I was waiting for the prince.

But I found him, my Moon. And he came with no slipper. Now I'm running lopsided, and I'm debating if I should keep hunting for the other heel that makes me feel like royalty or ditch it all and run barefoot through the forest not giving a fuck.

The latter appeals to me; a craving for freedom, for shedding convention. However, opposite me sits my Olea, still requiring my presence for years to come. So how do I calm this need to run barefoot in the constant summer, when I have to stay grounded to these hugging clouds of November?

Days dwindle early; I admit this is my least favored time of year. I understand that perspective shapes reality, and imagination is all we truly own. How can I turn this into something good and find joy even in my grief of not knowing who the hell I really am or who I want to become?

Deep within, there stirs something magnificent; a quiet force gathering strength not quite in bloom. It's like a seed taking root, its potential not yet visible, as it seeks nourishment from the soil of my experiences. Weariness settles in, my companion in the darkness. I've lingered here far too long, a familiar space where life fades into nothingness and desires wither like petals.

Who do I want to become? The question echoes in my thoughts as an invitation to reshape my identity. It's a tantalizing prospect to be anyone I choose. Yet, this freedom feels overwhelming when deciding what to eat poses a challenge. Meanwhile, my body swells, resisting my attempts to contain it within familiar boundaries. My pants grow tight and my favorite dress snug. I've even cut my wild hair and traded my smudged glasses in for new clear ones. I wonder if the old frames held a touch of magic. This ring I wore reminded me of abundance and my right to want something different than what I've been given. Shifting, growing still, it's unsettling when you still feel buried under the floor.

I don't feel unsafe, but I do not feel at home either. Instead, I'm adrift; neither flying nor sinking. At this crossroads of creation, I must decide whether to continue forward, fueled by trust in myself; or ignite a fire that consumes it all, leaving a trail of ashes behind. Something must shift, like tectonic plates beneath the surface of my existence.

Amidst this turmoil, I recognize the presence of support. It's a lifeline I've leaned upon for so long, but now, I wish to stand independently—no more codependency. I am now forging my own path. So, I'm making my own glass slipper, melting the shattered glass of time passed to find what it means to be in the unknown of becoming me.

MOONBEAM WRAPPED LOVERS

I came to this earth not to be a warrior
but to be a lover.
I'm not in my king era,
I'm in my *beauty era*.
Adoration.
Manifestation.
Feel the callings of what I desire
reach them like holy lovers.
Clasping hands
like the moonbeams wrap the waves.
Into her arms, echoing in a forever resonance—
this is my mastery.

I'm a new woman
at full capacity.
Brimming with the overflow;
I've finally found it again.

I touched it two years ago.
But now, this time,
it's here to stay;
stable inside my body.
No longer nested in the apartment
with just 300 square feet.
Or the access to the owl
watching over me;
In the park nearby,
nor in the lightness.
I feel like floating just two inches
above the grip of death
that kept threatening
to call my life to the grave before it's time.

Get ready or not, because this time,
I've learned how to come endlessly.
This promise in my flesh
I keep building; it's here that realities are made.
And this one is meant for creating
new soil for many to finally feel
the depths of infinite growth
as I keep practicing it.
For me.
For you.
For us.
I merge into the unknown,
and whisper into the parts of you
aching to breathe life.
Declaring it's time, my dear,
it's time you remember,
you are powerful.

Magican

IMAGINATION IS
THE BEGINNING
OF FREEDOM

I AM NO LONGER A WARRIOR I AM A MAGICIAN

WE CALL IT HEAVEN

In the infinite existence, we grapple with a fundamental question—when is it enough? Which holds greater power: desire or knowledge?

Attach to desire, and you'll win past logic every time. Every pattern of humanity's self-perpetuated web will tell you so. Take, for instance, our insatiable appetite for processed foods that harm our bodies, yet we continue to consume them. Within my marriage to Micah, I'd often stay up late eating a whole sheet of cookies I made or an entire bowl of hummus and pita chips, often feeling disgusting afterward. We're aware of the detrimental effects and the rise in chronic diseases. Yet, we succumb to the allure of convenience and instant gratification.

Similarly, we find ourselves entangled in toxic relationship dynamics, repeating cycles of trauma and heartbreak; even though we know deep down that we deserve better. I get it. It took me a decade to leave mine. And let's not forget the poisons disguised as quick fixes, promising miraculous results that slowly erode our well-being. It's a perplexing phenomenon—knowingly embracing self-destructive choices driven by the overpowering force of desire.

Yet, even this understanding becomes a hurdle, a step we find ourselves stuck on.

We devour foods that harm us, entangle ourselves in traumatic cycles that bind us, and fall prey to promises of toxic allure.

We have become addicted to the wrong desires. And I contemplate: can we reshape it all?

This reality we inhabit is one of self-destruction.

I continuously question why we endure suffering.

Then, I see it in my own hands; the repetitive patterns, the cycle of destruction and pain.

Except, I've shifted huge stones as I declared to Micah that day with the sunlight breaking through our backyard trees, how I was done. It felt like a powerful shift in finally choosing myself over trying to earn his love. As the first woman in a line of many women trapped in the cycle of toxic marriages, unable to break free from the grip of trauma bonding, I took the brave step to set myself free. I have relinquished the chains that bound me and stepped into a life where I am cherished, not for my ability to fix but for the beautiful essence of who I am.

No longer defined by the roles I played or the expectations placed upon me, I have reclaimed my individuality and discovered the power of self-love. It is a transformative journey of embracing my worth and creating a life where love flows freely, unencumbered by the chains of past traumas. By releasing myself from the cycle, I am rewriting my story and shaping a future filled with authentic connection and genuine love.

Yet, I crave further transformation. In my new blended family, I've felt powerless against values I can't alter.

In my marriage to Moon, our home became my greatest investment. We'd reach many points where I got tired of a certain way we existed and would implode to finally share how I felt about how things were going. It always threw Moon off guard because he showed me everything was okay, but I kept trying to be okay with a different value. In the middle of every conversation, we returned to having different values. It often felt like we'd reach a middle, and then we would slip back into programmed ways, leading to us not living in the middle together.

So, I kept asking, "How do you mend a patient who continuously undoes the stitches?"

Albert Einstein defined insanity as doing the same thing repeatedly and expecting different results.

I often wanted to quit, and to fall into my deeply ingrained pattern of saying, "I cannot."

Yet, my mentor's wise words echoed in my mind, "Build the bridge. Be the magician who transforms the wretched into something magnificent."

Be the one who gazes at the storm and declares, "Peace, be still."

I have achieved this within myself. I have performed this in my own life now, taking baby steps in seeing the messages we live aren't just rules for our girls but deep passions we witness to make their lives beautiful. They are shifting slowly with us, but it's required more patience as I learned building bridges requires new skills I had to acquire. Now, I crave that shift for the world we can create. But damn, it feels lonely.

Surrounded by others who seek escape in the name of healing, I yearn to cry out, "Stay present. Remain here!"

And yet, I, too, abandon myself while others move on to the next distraction. I left a part of myself wounded, a sacred part as if she never existed. Every time Micah declared that he didn't want to be married to me, I would make myself smaller, hoping it was then that he would come to love me. Still, I lost a part of myself every time I did that. In the end, he had nothing to know either.

Thankfully, all those parts are now reclaimed as I wrestled with my own demons. I turned and flipped out of familiar patterns into intentional living. I desire to reshape this world, not out of ego or control, but because I am exhausted by suffering, which is deemed normal. I am weary of settling for mere adequacy. I am tired of unnecessary pain. I may oversimplify, as I am prone to do.

It took over a year for Moon and I to come together to find our values in the middle, shed old habits, and build a family together, along with the support of outside people. Still, it took me frequently voicing what wasn't okay and saying, "I have to keep growing, and I hope you come with me. However, it has to be your choice to come."

Our bridge, for a moment, looked like me having to step away and declare I cannot rescue him and I cannot live in the spaces he keeps calling normal. In the end, I found true partnership to be when you both show up to grow together, do your work, and take responsibility for the places you've turned a blind eye to.

But what would it look like if we collectively transcended our limitations? What if we shattered the barriers that keep us trapped in needless suffering? Imagine a world where emotional regulation was instilled in us from a young age, our bodies and minds thrived in vibrant health, and greed was replaced with genuine compassion. Envision a reality where the basic needs of every individual were met and trauma became a distant memory. We would all embrace our innate creative powers in this marvelous world, growing in joy, magic, and wonder. It may seem like an unimaginable dream, but we yearn for it deep down.

I don't think we can even fathom such a world but we label it "Heaven," as if death will be the plot twist to bring us to the reality we all yearn to create. Instead, we wallow in the mud of shame and greed, wondering why we are always dirty with suffering. Surprised that our skin seems gone, our reflections have become unrecognizable buried beneath the layers we've accumulated. We have forgotten what it truly means to be fully alive, in soul and spirit.

The truth is that Heaven lies within our grasp; shedding complacency that settles for mediocrity, releasing the shackles of societal conditioning. As I strive to radiate with all my might, I hope that somehow, someday, you will discover the boundless magic within your grasp. Recognize the intrinsic beauty that resides within each of us and truly comprehend, deep within your bones, that everything else is worth uprooting.

PICKLED CHURRO

The sailboat suspended just for a moment right between his collarbone and chin framed perfectly by the sky. It was one of those transcendent artistic moments you wanted to paint and put up on your mantel. Moon and I laid on a beach blanket watching boats pass on the nearby river just thirty minutes from our now-shared home. We had decided to stop at one more beach before driving home after camping for a night.

During our trip, Moon enjoyed a day of kayak sailing with a friend, while I searched for the perfect spot to hang my hammock. With a nagging infection, I wasn't up for paddling.

After dropping Moon off at the boat launch near one of the inlets nestled between the islands of Olympia, Washington, I drove to their final destination in hopes of meeting them for lunch. Crossing the bridge of glittering morning water in forested two-lane roads, I arrived at their final destination, an island with a twenty-minute drive time. Slowing down to fifteen miles an hour, I puttered past camping spots and a camp host, where I found the day parking. There were trails to different edges of the island, more hike-in camping spots, and different boat launches. I hoped I could find a place to set up a hammock, nestle with my journal, and a book to read while I waited for Moon to arrive.

Strolling around this little island, through different forested paths and other campsites, I dead-ended each time at a boat dock or at the last empty camping spot. Feeling uninvited to any of these areas, I left in utter frustration not being able to find what I had hoped for, just two good ole trees to tie my hammock to. None existed here, so I opened Google Maps until I found another recreation area with a softer shoreline.

Overwhelmed between feeling out of place, unsure where to go, and what time Moon and his friend would arrive at the first island, I spent two hours looking for a hammock spot. Exhausted from the infection I was battling, I talked myself up to hiking down a trail to a sandy waterfront spot where I could finally tie up my hammock and hopefully relax.

Walking down, I felt my energy leaving me with each step. I tried to tap into wonder, noticing the beautiful ferns growing, the dew lingering on the leaves, the birds singing in the background, and the growing volume of waves on the water ahead. But wonder seemed far, as pain radiated through me with every pound of my feet against the dense soil beneath my hiking shoes. Determined to relax, I reached the bottom of the trail where everything opened up to a sandy beach on the water.

However, it was lined with seaweed and algae with flies buzzing off the heat of rotting ocean bodies, and the rain threatening to spittle itself all over me at any moment. Nonetheless, I set up my hammock and tried my best to enjoy the little bit of beauty I could muster myself to notice in this moment. I feel so often that I force myself into enjoying things. When I look back, I wish I'd just given myself a moment to be frustrated, scream in the car, and pout, instead of forcing myself to enjoy what I did have. I did eventually, but it bottled itself repeatedly in me, wanting to have it together more than I truly do.

While camping maybe wasn't the best of ideas in the first place, I'd battled so many years of feeling stuck at home because I was sick. I wouldn't let yet another month-long infection ruin living my life. So we went camping anyway. Despite my best efforts to enjoy the trip, depression and negativity snuck up on me like an ex-lover who keeps promising you they'll love you well this time.

I stayed in the hammock for thirty minutes before it began to rain, laughing and fuming in my head about how annoyed I was. But I kept trying to hold it together. I hated how much I always felt angry about how "bad things" were happening to me, when it seemed like my fault for not focusing on the good. How sneaky these toxic positivity moments can creep in when I was perpetuating my grief by not letting my anger and frustration fully express themselves in these building moments.

My anger built up to grief as the rest of the trip went on. I met Moon and his friend for lunch and then back at the original inlet. Moon and I went back to our spot, and I held in my feelings for what I'd experienced. I shared just little bits about the annoying things that did happen, while trying to share how nice it was to sit in the hammock for thirty minutes of the four hours he was having the time of his life with his old friend.

Later that night, we walked hand in hand. We strolled the campsite we stayed at, enjoying the night's evening stars, and nestled together once it got too chilly. Holding so much in, everything gave way to a familiar track of just wanting to give up.

Yet, I'd remember Olea, and these two other sweet step-daughters. I couldn't give up now. My Olea deserves her mommy whole. She's my fire to remember how to breathe above water when the ocean's darkness beckons me with relief from all the pain.

She's gone half the week, and while I'm delighted to have more alone time with my Moon, ache fills me when missing her.

However, Moon's smile lights up my world. His touch, hugs, laughter, and words shift everything for me, but they do not stop the pain. I press it down and try my best to enjoy the time without needing to regulate her and myself. This life of divorce is the most freeing, and heartbreaking experience.

In contrast, when you land in the depths of depression, everything aching inside you piles up; declaring this is the time we're going to bring up everything.

The mirror no longer looks like me. I've been a shell missing its life, just like the memory of sound when you press it hard enough against your ear.

Just thirty minutes from home, I finally let this depression rage before Moon and I cuddled up on the beach shore.

I found a cool spot in the sand and filled my ears with the punk rock flare of my heart, playing a song called "I'm Not Okay." I closed my eyes and let my body move in all its aches, in all the ways it desired. Part of me felt ridiculous thrashing about behind a bush on the beach. So I paused to open my eyes. I wondered how many people were staring at this absurd woman flaring her arms about like someone at a concert with no band or audience?

Isn't it funny how some movements fit in at the right venue, but seem off in other places? We can eat pizza with our hands, but not pancakes or cinnamon buns. What rules have we all agreed to that limit us from fully experiencing life?

At that moment, letting all the anger shift out of my body through movement, I finally felt the depression leave me. I began thrashing my arms about. I danced like I was at an emo band concert, jumping up and down and pretending to scream as I listened to a song with a chorus declaring what I felt, "I'm not okay. I'm not okay. Well, I'm not okay, I'm not o-fucking-kay."

Sometimes emotions do not need our soothing words or stuffing further behind noticing "pretty things." Sometimes they just need to be expressed.

My body has held so much rage; anger at what I've experienced and all the harm I ever faced. I have a right to be angry and let it out safely. I wish I'd done it in the comfort of my own home, but I wasn't giving myself the space to do that. So I found the only moment I could, there on that beach.

This depression calls me often. I always aim above ground despite my need to sit in the night's darkness, staying up late at night writing, raging, weeping, and grieving. The night illuminates all that's on my heart. It's too tangled for anyone else to unknot.

> Sometimes, our emotions must pickle
> like the cucumber in vinegar;
> let it mull over.
> It needs to sit in the jar,
> rattle,
> prattle,
> and cackle
> until the knot
> of our emotions
> is ready to fall loose
> into the truths it needs to express.

Shame creeps in often when I'm processing, declaring in a valley girl's voice, "You're just entitled. You should just quit if you cannot enjoy all of this now that you're finally here," thinking that now that I have a man who can cherish me means that I should be "all better and happy now."

But I see it's not that. This battle is wrestling with life when it all feels vinegared and soured despite the sweetness you're showered in, like kisses from Moon every day, giggles with our girls, and living room dance parties.

So, I tell Shame with all the confidence I can muster up, "Please don't call me entitled; I prefer the name 'Pickled Churro.'" I'm learning what it means to turn all that's been sour in my life into something absolutely sweet.

I hope one day to feel more like a fruiting tree one day. How do we become organic when you're seemingly made up of bottled poisons handed down from generation after generation? Remind me what it's like to juice like the apple, as I sip her, asking to become her very cells, fruiting.

Often, others hear my stories naming my will to live as "bravery wings." But I am no more a magician than the mirror I hold up for you. Behind it, some days I feel like a beast about to devour everything I love because this searing inside me won't stop its blood from dripping. Self-sabotage has a funny way of destroying everything we want because we have not accepted we are worthy of having it all; I've often felt that with my new family of five. There is more surrendering to do.

Moon's presence beside me on that beach, with the sailboat drifting through the frame that his head and collarbone created, reminds me of the essence of living a life unburdened by past shadows. It's a lot like sailing. You need to let the wind carry you, trusting its flow. Then, you must trust the pull of ropes. You carefully choose which ones to adjust and which ones you effortlessly let go of just when you think you should grip tighter.

We all have the power to turn all the wretched in our lives into whatever reality we wish. Often, I feel too twisted up. But somehow, when I lean into everything my soul has been calling me into, with every step of my life, I find I'm not knotted. I'm really learning to surrender my attachment to what I think I need to force myself into, and instead, like the sailboat giving into the wind of releasing more of this story I've been told is who I am.

JOY DWELLING IN PUMPKIN SCOOPERS

He slipped the misshapen orange plastic Halloween pumpkin scooper back into the ceramic stoneware we all have on our counters. You know, the one that holds the tall spoons, too big for the silverware drawer but used enough not to be tucked away high on the shelf?

I giggled at the thought that Moon, of all people, would use a pumpkin scooper that's been accidental. Now, a funky extreme scoop shape melted too many times, named as the "perfect tool" to stir Maddie's favorite food: pasta. He's always seeing the best in people and animals, looking past their imperfections and rough edges, and admiring that they are "always trying their best." It's a sentiment that has pushed me past my own edges, my quick judgments I've used as my safety shield, and opened me up to disarm and see a beautiful, incredible world we live in—just like he does.

While this pumpkin scooper-turned pasta spoon holds a story and a touch of sentimentality, I wonder how many of us cling to the bent, the misshapen, and the clearly worn-out pieces when we could have anything else.

BLOOMING UPSIDE DOWN | MAGICIAN

Yet, I can still hear his voice in my head, brimming with delight as he talks about how this pumpkin spoon is all he needs, with its perfect little triangle holes and clawed edges. The memory of his girls using it to scoop the goop out of the most adorable jack-o-lantern still lingers, etched in his mind like a cherished keepsake.

As much as it carries nostalgia, I can't help but argue that just because something was once valuable doesn't mean it needs to continue in use, much like the plastic steamer he used in the microwave, which I swiftly tossed out once I moved in due to its infusion of plastic into everything it cooked.

The pumpkin scooper held quirkiness and a story for Moon and his two girls. It brought a moment of sparked joy to pick out something odd in a container where it "shouldn't be," and be delighted when you reach in to manage your cooked pasta to find this funny orange tool that stood out amongst all the other items in the utensil jar. However, the pumpkin scooper had to leave our kitchen just like the plastic steamer. Its adorableness was causing the plastic to melt into the pot, which was clearly unhealthy.

To hold something new, we have to let go of something else. I keep wondering what keeps us hanging on to the things we find sentimental, holds a sliver of joy for us, and poisons us with every repeated immersion.

Is it the scarcity that joy is so rare it has to dwell only in the contorted?

I felt this as I stayed married to Micah for over a decade. When you love with all you have, it is easy to handle staying in love with the things harming you. He wanted out of our marriage so often. Still, I felt so deeply, and so passionately in love with him and our family that I was convinced this had to work out. Indeed, if I thought this amount of joy and love in all the good times, such as when we'd fill our living room with his record player playing Ray Lamontagne as we danced around in silliness with Olea at age three, it meant that it was okay to keep trying harder to make things work.

Letting Micah go, just like we had to let go of the beloved pumpkin scooper poisoning me more than nourishing my soul, allowed Moon into my life. My experience of love and joy wasn't limited to that relationship with Micah. It wasn't limited to that one marriage. It was inside of me, ready to touch whatever I wanted.

What if joy is as abundant as the waters of the rivers? How much will you allow yourself to experience, knowing joy's existence already dwells inside your cells?

DEPRESSION'S WOMB

Depression holds me in the womb of her darkness. I beckoned with an escape plan, "Let's end it. That cliff looks perfectly high."

But gravity anchors me down, whispering in her daily gentle caressing, "Stay, my dear, stay."

I wonder if when we lie down, it isn't always because we're exhausted but because our whole body wants to feel the hold of gravity intimately. When I was battling P.O.T.S. symptoms more severely, I often found myself being forced to sit down. And I think of this now, as a yoga teacher ending classes in Savahsanan or corpse pose, as we relax our whole bodies into the earth, maybe sometimes, to feel our connection back to the earth we need to feel gravity hold more of us than just our feet. Sometimes, I wonder if P.O.T.S. just showed me we need more connection. With this in mind, I promised myself, in this deep state of depression, that I wouldn't leave this tent.

As Moon and I embarked on our week-long anniversary camping trip in the pristine wilderness of Northern Washington, we ventured into an untamed landscape that was not always accessible or accommodating, especially for those of us who preferred the cozy comforts of home. Our version of camping held a cache of creature comforts, including a cozy bed with an assortment of pillows piled high to fill up our tent, a six-inch-thick mattress pad, and my iPhone with its battery life waning, replicating the soothing sounds of rain for me to fall asleep to.

Yet, as our days in the wild progressed, I could sense the creeping darkness of depression beginning to overshadow the serenity of nature. The numbness took hold, and I contemplated an escape; a way out. It's a place where depression often leads me, where I feel as if the quickest solution might just be to leave this world forever. As Moon hiked down to the restrooms, I promised myself I wouldn't leave the tent after depressions slammed me down.

I recently read that our minds, in heightened emotions, look for a quick solution to a problem and make a quick judgment. This default pattern has helped us evolve in making quick decisions to stay alive through so much. For example, when we are angry at a sandwich not fitting inside a plastic bag, it's often not the fact that the bag is a piece of crap, but the underlying emotion of frustration is actually overwhelming. The sandwich not fitting is the tip of the iceberg of all the emotions we've felt that day, week, or month, as life is spilling out and exploding in that moment. So, while it's easy to blame the plastic bag maker for not being the right size for standard sandwiches, the real problem is not having the capacity to fully express all the emotions inside us.

Still, we must learn to double-check when it comes to complex trauma responses because under one emotion can be two more tied to memories that have yet to surface, or even energy that doesn't have a name, as we faced it at such a young age when we didn't have context for what was happening around us. But deep inside, we knew something was wrong as we responded with a survival tactic.

My escape route from depression has been used so much, that the grove inside the window to jump out of, in the towering building of my trauma, feels increasingly tempting each time the grief and weight of life come knocking at my door.

"Anchor into gravity. Let her hold you. I promise. I promise this will get better. You have a purpose. Stay. Please stay." I hear a wise voice in me say.

I try to convince myself to listen to her, this wiser part of me. Moon returns with his beanie and puffy red jacket covering his slender body. "We should go on a hike."

My body is exhausted, and I respond sheepishly, "You should just go alone. I promise I won't leave this tent to do anything stupid."

He unzipped the mesh door, pulled off his shoes, pushed the towering pillows aside, and sat with me. "I cannot leave you with that statement." He closed the mesh door, undid his coat, crawled under the blanket with me, and pulled me into hours of hugs as I laid intertwined between numbness and tears of hopelessness. I laid weeping in his arms for what felt like an hour. I wanted to push him away. But I let him love me as he stayed with me.

Slowly, with the continuation of his love, I'm learning what it means to receive the unconditional love that can just sit with you without fixing but holding you in a warm embrace; still feeling the depths of your emotions at the same time.

This womb of darkness and depression has an ugly side that threatens to tear out all of me, but it's here that she always holds a deeper call, "Come, come sit with me."

I refused and instead kept standing at the edge of my quick exit. Shouting back, "I have no worth. I have no value to this world. Please let me go."

It's then Olea, now nine years old, flashes before my eyes. Her pull is stronger than gravity.

I open photos of her in the little amount of life I have left in my iPhone battery and extend pictures of her. The laughter, her smile, her tricks on the couch, upside down in my backseat, hanging like a monkey everywhere. I pulled out enough and allowed sleep to soothe me while Moon and I laid cuddled.

At one point, Moon left the tent and began to make dinner. Numbness settled while I laid in the tent, watching him as the night turned pitch dark: walking around the picnic table, reheating soup, and eating under the pitch black sky.

The forecast said we could see the aurora borealis that night, so I decided that this would get me out of the tent. As more stars appeared, Moon invited me to go watch the stars. I donned my puffy jacket, beanie, and boots, slipped out of the tent, and reached for his hand as I mosied down the path where we could see more stars.

Soon, the Milky Way opened its curtain to its midnight showing. Moon and I walked down to the boat dock on the glacier-coated, tropical turquoise-colored river of the North Cascades, letting the stars saturate us with their leftover shine.

As we gazed up, I thought, "How bright are we to them? Do their light spectrum's see in a different range like birds see ultraviolet light?"

Our trip ended the next day, and I stayed in the womb of my depression for the next week.

Olea came home to me from Micah's with a small sore that progressed really fast into a full-blown infection. We had doctor visits and prescriptions, and every part of me was thrown back to the flashes of all the medical trauma that began with me at the beginning of my illnesses.

It, too, started with a rash that would not go away. After two years of trying every antibacterial, topical steroid, trial drug, diet change, removing every known chemical in our house, and frequency energy treatment, I felt like I had tried it all. Nothing helped, and everything got worse.

After visiting Dr. Jantz for my last cardiologist appointment, he recommended a beta blocker that helped other P.O.T.S. patients. I agreed to try it, but one side effect was yeast infections. I was never a fan of trying drugs that weren't made for the actual symptoms I was experiencing. But I tried it one day, and within one dose, I broke out in a yeast infection that lasted for nine months, becoming too non-responsive to any prescription the doctors gave me.

Then, there were the steroids that sparked the separation of me from the previous life I lived as a young mama and photographer. From the outside, it seemed with every use of medication, my health and life spiraled.

Could I trust Western medicine to cure my daughter when it seemed to only exacerbate and leave me completely hopeless as I had similar issues arise barely seven years before?

The fastest way to pull yourself out of a depression is to have to care for someone else. But maybe it's not. Perhaps it's actually the quickest way to draw out the truth of what set you deep into depression's womb in the first place. In the darkness, it all gets a deep cradling with desperate shouts, "Please hold me, see me, love me."

I couldn't trust what the doctors were saying, but I had tried everything else I knew. So I leaned on her dad, Micah. I called him on the way to pick up the prescription drugs I had been avoiding for twenty-four hours, hoping we'd find something else to help. "I cannot do this. This is all too close to what happened to me. I need you to decide if it's okay to give her this medicine. I don't want it to ruin her like it did me."

"I trust this is different. Olea has more support than you ever did," he replied on the phone.

While I sat in the underground parking garage of the medical facility after talking to Micah, I wept. I wept for all the times I couldn't trust this system built to heal us, this same system that seemingly failed me just as much as my family, who silenced and abused me.

I kept aching for a tribe. Someone to always have my back. When you get really sick, your support to make it through should be having a good care team, and for the first four years, I didn't have any of that when healing my body. There were just extremely kind humans doing what they were trained to do: diagnose, write a prescription plan, and treat the disease.

My experience with doctors in Western society hasn't been healing systemic issues, but managing broken pieces in a juggling act. I didn't want to be managed. I wanted to heal. I didn't stop searching for healing.

I found it through a quirky man, Anthony Williams, amplifying a return to fruits and vegetables and a physician in New York City, Dr. Greene, who had Lyme disease and cured herself by trying it all. She knew her training as a surgeon and physician wouldn't be able to fix all she'd been experiencing. So she tried everything until she landed on this same quirky character and his information about healing the body with fruits, vegetables, herbs, and avoiding foods that cause more trouble than nourishment.

In all my reflections on being sick, I always skipped to this part of my story—finding Dr. Greene. Yet, inside this womb of depression, she came to tell me of the trauma I hadn't fully released in my own body.

I felt lost those first two years. Each physician was so caring and kind. I set my hope in them to rescue me. Deep down, I think, "Maybe they will love me enough to help me thrive." They all wanted to each time I sat on their crinkly-covered beds with disposable paper.

Each physician who treated me, from my dermatologist, rheumatologist, cardiologist, gastroenterologist, and gynecologist, wanted so beautifully to help me. They, too, wanted answers and found none. I wanted to believe them. I wanted to trust them but couldn't because they never provided the healing I needed. Yet, they didn't know about my traumatic birth with Olea. They didn't realize how helpless I felt with all I'd been through throughout my life. I felt like my skin was being peeled off when she was born, and then it did just that. So they did what they knew how to do: test, test, test, prescribe, test, prescribe.

My body shouted its reply when it felt quieted, always with an exclamation in all the rare side effects such as year-long co-infections and joint crystallization. And then, it wasn't until I felt empowered over my life that I felt the courage to live. I was taking back my life that had been flipped on its head, saying, "This is still mine," as I entered a deeper layer of self-worth and nourishment. It was there that I began to heal.

The year I took my healing into my own hands, I dove deeper into my meditation practices, yoga, and plant nourishment, beginning to find my deep worth again. Surrounding myself with powerful coaches like Dr. Chelsea Page, therapists covered by insurance, poets, books on the body's wisdom and Trauma Bonding like The Betrayal Bond by Patrick J. Carnes, as well as learning new modalities of healing like Hatha Yoga, Yoga Nidra, and an intuitive somatic movement meditation called Kindrêd, that taught me how to embody what my inner self truly knew, but hadn't ever had context to become. I finally started to heal, little by little. This time, with a doctor who knew how to heal, and an entirely new tribe of powerful voices that helped me remember I was worth reaching for a life that was not just survival was absolutely stunning. It wasn't easy. It was three steps forward, two back. It was infuriating and isolating, but it was a tipping point that set me to the freedom of better understanding, not just the physical wounds my body experienced but the emotional ones, giving it the support it needed.

In all of this, I found that we often want to skip to the good or easy parts, like blaming the plastic bag maker and moving past all the ugly in our memories and bodies. Still, these moments come back up where we crumble. We want to crawl out, run as fast as we can in another direction, or even jump off a cliff.

However, sitting with gravity, we find this space in us that still needs to be held and shown: this time, it's different. This time, we know our worth. And it's with her tears of truth I know I can leave this womb of depression here and, this time, set up the placard to remind myself next time she calls me to visit, "Welcome. Here you come to listen, witness, and release. Something still needs its voice. Anchor yourself long enough to hear her ache. Give her a voice and truth of the power in your ability to create. This is just the beginning of your majestic beauty."

LIGHT ON THE EDGES

"Your illnesses were what you wished for." An audacious state-ment uttered to me as she sat in front of me with long, dark hair blowing in the ocean breeze. To some, it may sound horrendous to think that an illness could ever be desired.

I started this document when I was twelve, "All the fun things I'm going to do with my child." In it, I kept a running list of activities I'd want to do with my children one day. It included everything from science experiments to traveling to swinging on swing sets together. I wish I could find this document, but before the age of cloud storage, it got lost to the whims of switching computers, shared hard drives, and the unreliable length of a computer's lifespan.

Back then, keeping such a list felt normal to me. However, when I mentioned it to one of my therapists, she told me it was a unique thing to do. In hindsight, I wonder if the list was not just a future wish but also a longing for the experiences I wished I had with my mom.

I have a few sweet memories with her: cuddling before bed, doing my sister Sara and I's hair, singing in the car on the way to church, shopping sprees where I would hide in between the clothing rack and jump out to scare her just when she couldn't find me. I'd laugh, but she just sighed in exasperated fear. On a phone call once, as I was driving home from a photography shoot in Denver with regular thirty-minute car rides, she told me, "Your sister always stayed close to me. But you were just this other thing. Always finding laughter, wanting to explore, seeking adventure."

I always wanted to try everything except the weird-looking dinners. You know, the 'adult foods' that aren't chicken nuggets, grilled cheese, french fries, or, you know, typical kid food? I was adventurous until then.

Being a mother myself, I can see that this list I made wasn't just what I wished my mother did with me, but this deep desire in me for the mother I wanted to be—fully present. My mother did her best, as all mothers do, but she wasn't home after school. We went to babysitters, or I was home alone with Sara. Our family vacations were often with other people and/or in a setting where we had "kid things" to do with babysitters. We had activities, our lives were brimming full, and rarely just sat around talking.

As I grow older and understand my own needs better, good listening skills have become crucial for anyone close to me. They need to have a genuine desire to listen deeply. I would like to know if my mother ever truly knew me or even had the capacity to do so. It's something she was never fully capable of. With my daughter, I cherish moments like sitting across from each other at the table, turning down the music in the car to talk, going for walks, and allowing her to ramble on about whatever is on her mind. My ears are the endless wells for her deepest thoughts.

My daughter is still a mystery to me, and I never want to claim that I fully know her. That assumption would hinder my journey of remaining open to her ever-changing growth.

Sometimes, we want to know things to move on quickly to other things. This critical skill in our minds is vital for our survival: remembering how to walk every day, how to speak the language we use the most often, and how to feed ourselves. Yet, we use this too often in our relationships. Using our knowledge to make assumptions about the other. It's there that we get into the most trouble. It's where we lose our passion for the other. Inside curiosity lies the unknown and sparks the desire to keep discovering. It's our basic human biology.

However, with relationships, it's one we have to keep cultivating. It's one I want to forever do with all my beloved and all of humanity. The old phrase of assuming will always stand true. "When you assume, you make an ass out of you and me."

Once, I was exploring a beach on the Oregon coast that requires you to walk through a cave. I noticed the similarities of this experience with trauma. The air was dark and damp from the sea air around me. The wall touched the ocean, not just through the molecules floating in the air, but recently as the king tides lifted life past their usual edge more profoundly into the depths of typically dry land. The caves are dark, especially when they are long tunnels. They hold a peculiar life in that they usually include at least one end with light. If you fix your eyes on the light, you cannot easily see the floor or walls. But, if you close your eyes and avoid the light, your eyes will adjust. This is an interesting metaphor for where we all land in our own dark night of the soul.

Often, throughout my years of battling chronic illnesses, sharing with anyone about what I've been through, or even what I deal with daily, I get the reply, "I don't know how you do it."

Here's the thing, you cannot because your eyes haven't adjusted to life in the dark. It doesn't necessarily get more accessible, but our human biology is made to adapt. These horrific challenges that some of us have to overcome aren't done overnight. We only become visible to the world once we reach a baseline sense. Yet, it's there in the darkness that I realized I have received everything I've ever asked for.

Deep in meditation, I'll often use my real-life experiences to catapult me into a profound subconscious journey. And I did the same with this coved beach, only accessible through a cave. As I dove into a meditation, I saw a light with soft billowing branches holding the threshold of the cave's outlet, and the beginning of something else entirely at the end of the cave's darkness. I pushed aside the branches, and before me unraveled a tumble of rocks singing as the waves glided around, above, and in between each of them. Surround sound held the cliff edges framing the ocean. Sea rocks scattered off in the distance, some rocks jagged-sharp pointing straight up and some smoothed over perfect for perching atop. Warm air surrounded me with a cooling breeze pulled in by the waves. Beneath my feet, I felt the cool water kiss my toes and slide off as if to greet me hello. Off the edge of one of the sea rocks was a woman with long brown hair and bare feet, gazing peacefully off into the distance. Her knees bent in as she held her shins. Her eyes were closed, clearly lost in the magic of this place. As soon as I turned towards her, she shot up like a best friend seeing you for the first time in years.

She quickly hopped off the rock and ran on the sand to greet me. Grabbing my hand, she was full of smiles. She led me up to the rock she was sitting on. She gave me the biggest hug and then touched my heart. I followed suit. It's there that our souls connected in messages without words. My whole body rushed full of energy as if I were lights on a Christmas tree that just got plugged in, every nerve ending filled up with sheer joy. Without words, I felt her say, "I feel your grief for the mother you didn't have. Let yourself grieve her. I see you wanted to experience something different. But don't you see, what you deeply desired, you have become for your daughter? You are the mother you wanted to experience."

Tears began to slide down the edges of my eyes similar to a recently watered succulent. Its leaves do not absorb moisture. It glides directly down to its core roots. I wanted to rebuttal and say that I wasn't there for my Olea; how my illnesses stole so much. But before I could formulate my usual reply, she told me, "In the best you could, in all you saw, your illnesses became how you stayed with her."

In this twisted understanding, I'm now seeing this too. I knew this woman was right; spot on, bull's eye. It felt like my mother was always working. She wasn't home after school to play, make us snacks, or even help us with our homework. I often went to my neighbors' or friends' houses and would stay for dinner. Their mothers didn't play with us either. But having them home with their warmth and love felt different from my house, which often felt empty, even with the TV my family always had on.

Deep inside me, I have this passion for changing the world. For doing great things in a career, but illnesses halted my work two years after my daughter was born. I got so sick I had to close my successful wedding photography business, trying to mother, run a business, and occasionally travel across Colorado on weekends. I was on track to become very successful, busy, and unavailable to experience life with my daughter. I knew this. I felt it deeply, and then suddenly, I didn't have to.

The year I closed my businesses was one of the most brutal years of my life, being so sick and undiagnosed. I was living in doctors' offices for tests, and not having the self-care management tools I have now. Yet, looking back, I see photos and videos of all the fun my, at the time, three-year-old daughter and I got to have. We explored local rivers, played forever in the backyard, had tea parties, dressed up, baked, and did all the beautiful things you can do with little ones. Of course, there were the days I'd be counting down the clock until her dad would get home. There were days I had to ask friends to come to watch her because I couldn't get out of bed without passing out. There were days I could not hold her because the pain was so bad. But these illnesses gave me a childhood back with her.

I see more than ever how these illnesses that I thought kept me from so much brought me the present, abundant life I wanted with my daughter. Years later, I no longer need illness to help me stay present with her. I can drive my daughter to school, play after school, travel with her, go on adventures, play "tickles," read stories, cuddle, bake together, dance, and play dress up. So I soak up each moment I can get with her. It's not perfect. Some days, I get exhausted from "mommying" and want to lock the bathroom door and let no one in. Now, I see her half-time with the divorce, so I find ease in being more fully present with her when she's in my arms.

However, these illnesses have taught me to slow down, learn self-awareness, and do the emotional work I've gone through to discover the unhealthiness of my inherited biology and relationship skills. It's taught me how to listen to my body in ways few ever learn. It sheds light on all the edges that are easy to ignore when you're on the outside looking in. It's taught me how to be more compassionate and understand the depths of suffering we all experience. I could spend a lifetime explaining how illnesses lead me to the most tender places.

So, it's no longer with anger that I shed my need for illnesses but with a tenderness of gratitude for the journeys it has led me through. I still wouldn't wish it upon anyone, but I lean into the tension of the truth that suffering stretches us when we maybe wouldn't have otherwise. It's with the jagged darkness we're cut open and discover we weren't bleeding from the new wound, but all the old ones that were too easy to ignore otherwise.

I wept more with this woman on the sea rock in my meditation. Her hand pressed against my chest, helped me see these truths. Then, she asked if I was ready to let them go. I nodded, and she began her work. As if I had a redundant nervous system, these glittering gold strings were pulled out of me. She then held them in her hand and gently blew on them. They flew into the air and turned into black birds flying off into the setting sun. She repeated this a few times until I thanked her. I got up from the rock and went back through the cave.

I opened my eyes in bed, still shedding tears of joy, relief, and mystery.

EDGES OF THE BLADE

Moon and I nestled into our hidden retreat behind the pine tree, just enough to shield ourselves from outside viewers in the condo complex. Even on the darkest night of the year, we could raise the blinds, basking in the glow of our own luminous skin. Our glowing skin is where the edge of darkness begins and ends. In the darkness, we cannot move by what we see but only by what we feel: sensations.

Stillness. It's the theme of this winter season. How is it that something is still when bodies never truly cease their pulse? By relinquishing sight we refrain from relying on knowledge to move. It is an existence at the edge, where only the senses of touch and deep belly trust can guide us in utter darkness.

Together, we ventured through the darkness, our bodies intertwining, carving new lines and shapes; until we, too, discovered the beautiful mysteries of getting lost in the abyss.

The solstice often beckons reflection, a slow dance of gratitude and thankfulness, releasing what no longer serves us and embracing the new.

Before immersing ourselves in darkness, we scrolled through photos from the past year. Among them, I stumbled upon a text. The words spilled out of me like glitter, illuminating everything around me reflecting a sparkling light. I feel distant from the person who once emanated such beauty.

In the past, it was often in this darkness that I would let my truth spill out when I lived alone. But now, in this life with my beloved Moon and our three daughters, our house is filled to the brim. There is nothing to spill out when darkness descends, only the exhaustion that lingers behind my eyes.

My body is learning a newfound level of safety, deeper than it has ever known outside the beautiful existence I share with him. Alongside this growth, I face challenges, forced to confront profound healing because I am no longer alone. Yet deep within me, I recognize that a piece of me had to dissolve for us to become one family. And in these moments of recollection, I often yearn for her: the one who lived alone.

I miss the woman who danced so freely at sunsets.

I miss the woman who penned sensible and nonsensical words, providing them a home beyond her flesh.

I miss the woman who adorned herself in clothes that made her feel like a queen.

I miss the woman who traipsed on a mountain almost everyday because it was her backyard.

None of her is untouchable again. Yet, she feels so far.

I feel like a shell closed off. I felt open before, and now I think all the locks are bolted tight.

Dr. Chelsea Page, my coach and therapist, wisely asked me during this season, "What if you need to be open to being closed?"

I wanted to revolt at her response, but I replied, "I hear you."

"Boundaries aren't a bad thing, you know."

It was a much needed reminder that we don't always have to stay in an expansive state. Seasons of healing flow like the seasons of our earth, sheltering within to deeply nourish and return to the soil; the roots of what allows us to keep blooming.

Trauma has resurfaced inside my body as if I was recently attacked. Survival mode flipped on, and all the tendencies to find safety outside me burned like a rash.

My usual creation of security feels numb. I can no longer dive into meditations as I once could.

I find my mind wandering to so many spaces. Have I let myself become too much, not of my own, in motherhood and becoming a wife again?

This season is asking me to go in and become a better listener. I thought I already was, but I heard her speak. "You've listened to some, but you mostly hear us and then ignore us. Mostly, you push past because you believe it exists outside of you. You will find everything you seek, my dear. When will you see what you've already deeply known? It's here, right here in you. Please stop pushing us away."

It's time to listen and respond to all she wants.

I wonder if I have let myself get swallowed whole in my relationship? I no longer know where I exist. The very things I promised myself—to not be engulfed in marriage and to not be swallowed by motherhood. Have both become true as I sit in the darkness again, striving to discover my edges. Where do I begin? Where do I exist? Where is my place that isn't defined solely by being his wife or their mother that isn't a title of belonging to another? I want a statement of being: this is me.

After getting married to Moon, I found myself putting on the old role of the mother and the wife I thought I had to be, even for Micah. I was always picking up, organizing, planning meals, making food, making sure kids didn't watch too much TV, and emotionally regulating everyone. And my god, I was exhausted from week one together as a family of five.

Moon asked me specifically not to pick up any of these roles. Still, he was working two hectic jobs while I was figuring out where my place in this world was after letting myself fall out of love with wedding photography, recovering from chronic illnesses, and where my love for helping others heal came into play.

I saw the opportunity to help our new little family become whole. This gift I have of seeing all the places of improvement and how, with little adjustments, so much more goodness can be experienced. Yet, to others, it is exhausting when layered on like too many coats a mother is insistent you wear when you go out into the snow.

So I had to slowly let each layer go, learn how to communicate my needs and my boundaries, and ask Moon to pick up more layers he was insistent he didn't need to carry.

It took us a year to balance ourselves out, but in the middle of it all, the lies of who I was supposed to be as a wife and mother had to become rewritten outside of the patriarchy that says women are to stay home, be responsible for emotions, and keep things tidy.

I had to become louder, bigger, and share more of my desires, as together, Moon and I balanced each other out. It also included me needing the womb of our bed to heal the lingering demons of trauma, and him stepping into his power to emotionally regulate the girls, too, after years of just saying this is who they are.

I believe this is the profound journey of women at this moment. How do we continue to become ourselves while existing within the relationships we deeply cherish?

I see those who are alone and have no partner to call beloved. I wonder how lonely they feel in the darkness of night. Do they lose their own edges, too?

The grass is always greener and more defined at an angle some distance away. The closer you get, the harder it becomes to discern where everything begins and ends. But if you go further out, no blade will stick out— it becomes a field.

What is the distance we must observe ourselves to know truly? Is it the distance that allows us to comprehend our definition? The distance where we can perceive ourselves not just as individuals but as an entire species? Or is it the near-sighted distance where only the close edges are defined?

I am: it is specified.

Such audacious statements require the commitment to continually view ourselves through new lenses and the willingness to discard the lenses we were told we must wear. We must have the flexibility to go too close and tumble out so far we remember the greatness of all that holds us to earth.

I'll look for my glasses that help definition come to life when things between six inches and infinity come into view. Since age twelve, I've needed their assistance in seeing the truth. I think maybe that's it—seeing ourselves through new lenses.

To find self is to forever commit to a new lens, instead of the one you were told you had to become. It is the listening and responding. It's not just the absorption of words. It means declaring, "This is my edge, and this is the darkness. I am both and neither simultaneously." So, take these new pairs of glasses. Together, we can see something new. Promise me never to stop looking for the six and sixty-six thousand inch views. In each one, you will discover your true self.

I am the blade.

I am the field.

This is me.

RENAMING THE REFLECTION

I slipped into a loose shirt, the fabric seemingly attempting to hide the bulge that had nestled between my eyes and toes. This body, holding so much within its cells, silently storing toxins, deserves my gratitude. But in some moments, I feel resentment at how much I don't feel at home.

These clothes, relics of a past version of myself, lay in my under-the-bed dresser as if shedding them would mean letting go of an integral part of me. A trip to a thrift store exposed my struggle to find anything that resonates with the present person I'm becoming.

But true solace wasn't found in those old clothes—it was in the moments of intimate connection with my beloved. Stripped down and vulnerable, societal standards and ill-fitting attire didn't matter. In my own skin, just alone, I finally felt at home.

However, looking in the mirror, I was surprised by a hatred I couldn't explain. With curiosity, I dove into the oceans of my consciousness through meditation to confront this grief. After so many years of anger, I've learned that anger is often hidden grief. Yet I couldn't get over the fact that now, of all times in my life, I loved myself more than ever before. So why did I feel this hatred?

The daily struggle became apparent. It was the memory of them, my family, that I faced each morning, not just my own. In mirrors, I saw their hurt and mine. They took parts of me before I could even understand my form. I wasn't the one to blame, but I carried their weight each day.

As I confronted this, my thoughts echoed with a simple question. "Is this why I rarely look in the mirror?" The reflection no longer reflected me; it mirrored them.

Their influence on my body had been so profound that my body ached with the weight of their transgressions. My jaw clenched in the night, and my chest tightened in response to the wounds I carried. The doctors recommended cleanses that felt like mere band-aids over an open wound.

Yet, a simple decision awaited. In this ocean meditation, I grasped my power—the power to rewrite my reality. With the stars as my witness, I vowed to reshape my existence by giving myself a new name and new identity entirely.

No longer clinging to the name my parents gave me, I embraced the name Lumalia. This name came as a spark of finding light and a reminder of affection from someone I dearly loved named Lia. Her birth came with a death of the stories of who I was and who she's leading me to be. I'll thank this past version of self for all the clever ways she's allowed us to survive as she begins to part. This isn't abandonment. This is reincarnation. Except, I'm skipping the part where you need ash and a morgue. I stepped into a space where I could release the pain, relinquishing the victimhood that had become my navigation. Lumalia symbolized an empowered woman who fashioned her reality based on her soul's calling while honoring the stories of her past lives.

Changing my name became pivotal—granting myself a new identity, free from the constant association with my family's abuse narrative. Lumalia was a break from the past, a journey toward re-membering my ability to choose who I get to be daily.

So, I cast aside the chains and the names that had bound me and suffocated me. Embracing Lumalia, I charted a course toward self-love, greeting each dawn with faith in my ability to transform—no longer defined by a history I had not chosen, but by the Lumalia I was destined to become: a woman shaped by her story yet empowered to create her own reality. This woman finally feels blissfully at home within herself.

NO LONGER YOUR ANGEL

I am no longer holding your
trauma because you called me your angel.

I am no longer holding your
suffering because you believed tears to be weak.

I am no longer holding your
pain because you were too afraid to see
it is the beginning of beauty.

I am no longer holding your
hand because you are too scared
of the sound of your own steps.

I am no longer holding you sacred
until you first discover it yourself.

I am no longer holding you to become
who I imagine you can be
because you deserve to hold
faith in your body
instead of mine.

I am no longer rescuing you
from the harm I see you stepping into.

I am no longer here to be
your savior.

I am holding myself
as angelic.
I am holding myself
as powerful.
I am holding myself
fucking boisterously.
I am holding myself
in deep belief.
I am holding myself
from repeating history.
I am holding myself
as the most powerful creator.

I am no longer subject
to this script of suffering
because I see it now
as an act of love
to let you continue
down your own path.

Hold your raging sword high
above your throat
fierce in your anger
to fight for all that is wrong,
while I take mine;
and discover its weight is light
because it is truly a wand.

Magician, you must call me
for I am magic
in everything I touch.

TOO BRIGHT

Despite all the healing I've experienced, the journey continues into discovering the depths of myself. When you've been on a rarer path, you sometimes notice extreme dualities in yourself. I found myself drawn to the depths of existence, yearning to touch both suffering and joy with the same intensity. I wondered how you hold such seemingly contrasting emotions when your fingers are like strainers, and your blood flows like a streaming waterfall carrying the weight of life's experiences.

I felt the ebb and flow of life's cycles, knowing that we are all interconnected—a part of the same circuit. There were moments when I touched the depths of suffering as I lost myself in the darkness. Strangely, I found a fondness for these moments, as if they reminded me of what it truly means to be alive. But even in my admiration for the depths, I yearned for a life without pain, a life where suffering would not cloud my existence. It always feels like I am asking the big life questions.

Out on a hike with Moon, we turned the trail's corner from the shades of evergreen trees into a sweeping valley as Mount Hood glistened her summer's glaciers in the background. Framed by wild-flowers sprinkled in purples, pinks, and yellows, rushing rivers echoed through the canyon, with the cliff's edges reminding you of your mortality. Standing before this majestic mountain, I felt a sense of reverence. The resolute and unwavering mountain spoke to me of its many seasons and truths. I wanted to know its wisdom, its strength in the face of storms it constantly coexists with, the joy and suffering, well at least what "we" call them.

Moon and I stood adoring her grandeur, but he soon had to turn away and squint his eyes as the dirt reflected the midday sun.

"Why can't you open your eyes?" I asked him.

"It's too bright." He replied, scrunching his face with his dark hair tied up in an endearing man bun.

"Everyone always has that problem, and I wonder why it is. It's never bothered me." I delight, unempathetically, like the ignorant human I sometimes am, as I stared straight ahead with my New Zea-land cap on, glasses with UV protection, and hair twisted in a braid resting on my shoulder.

My eyes were wide. I wanted to absorb every ounce of light and color dancing before me, beckoning this scene to change every cell inside of me to know her strength. Mount Hood stood before us, coated in her lingering glaciers dripping down her crevices, carving deeper truths of knowing so many seasons.

Whispering across the mountain, I asked her to reveal her secrets, her truth of standing strong amidst life's challenges. In my heart, I wondered if I was alone in my desire to be blinded by the brilliance of life, to fully immerse myself in the experience of existence while also deeply wishing for others to join me.

I realized that maybe this was the essence of my uniqueness, my willingness to embrace life in all its shades and hues. I longed for oth-ers to join me, to open their eyes and hearts, to dance and splash colors nonsensically. Together, we could be stronger and more resilient.

At that moment, I heard her say in reply, "Your strength grows in connection, in a shared resilience to let the wind shape you and trust that what you thought you needed to keep is actually holding you back from experiencing even more beauty than ever imagined. Grow tall and let it all gently shape you."

Ready to embark on guiding others to open deeply to both the joy and sorrow, I ask you, as I share my story—even if it seems too bright or too deep, will you join me with whatever hats, braids, and protection you need to come and learn that embracing life's fullness is always done better together?

SOME DAYS SHE CLOSES TOO

Today, they were closed: my neighbor's tulips. Their front yard was adorned with multiple varieties and daffodils, all coming into full bloom as spring's embrace unfolded over the Pacific Northwest. A month of additional sunshine, longer days, and the promise of warmer temperatures greeted us in early April.

But then, an unprecedented storm swept through, leaving behind inches of snow. The initial bloom had paused in what we jokingly called the "third winter" of this season. The warmth, the vibrant blossoms; none are fully here anymore. They peaked out, but today, as the clouds hover over us like a blanket, I'm a little bit tired of being smothered as I wish for my skin to taste the warmth of the sun again.

Painted by this scene, I've realized, I feel mirrored by the tulip, opening and closing, on my journey to bloom. Much like her, I yearn to remain open, yet she whispers the rhythms of connectedness to the earth—a cadence I can all too easily forget, while confined within the worlds we construct.

And so, I learn. As the tulip breeds underground, sprouting fresh from their bulbs, I also seek to root myself. They start with a quiet green, allowing the hue of life to gradually emerge. With each sun-kissed day, and a touch of warmer rain, she unfurls each petal as a testament to her patient unfolding.

In the past, I assumed blooming was a linear process: always open, always reaching. Now though, I observe the tulip closing on certain days; as if she, too, retreats—a behavior mirroring my heart as it closes for days of deep sustenance after navigating so much this life calls us to face. It's as if the clouds welcomed us both to take a moment to rest. This is a time for nourishment.

Witnessing the tulip pull in her petals all day long reminds me of times I've drawn myself in, wanting solace in the middle of many expressions.

Even now, with my family of five, I sometimes close all the doors and windows to my home, step outside, and seal the sounds of my family happily inside. I sit under the willow tree that hangs over our neighbor's backyard. And like the dew, I imagine myself like the tulips, letting just the droplets drip in between her petal's slips. I think of the tears I've shed alone, my own form of dew hydration. It's there in the cocoons. I think we both get a rarely celebrated form of nutrition.

Just then, as anticipated, the transformative moment arrives—the full expression of her lips utterly parted when she unfurls: the part, the expansion, the whole explosion of color. It resonates with those times when I've surrendered myself to the beauty inside myself, no longer hiding her but letting her be fully witnessed by myself.

I've learned that just as the tulip reaches her peak, followed by shedding her petals, I, too, experience cycles of growth and release. There's a bittersweet beauty in letting go and returning to the earth of my own being, ready to sprout anew.

However, unlike other flowers, the tulip has a trick. She multiples by herself, duplicating underground where no one is looking, until she has sprouted again next year. This time, not with only one stem—but many. I feel a kinship with her resilience and her ability to regenerate without seeding. Her unique growth reminds me that change isn't always visible and that sometimes it's not about spreading seeds as far as you can, but about trusting the roots you're building to multiply beyond imagination.

So, I'll keep watching her each year. Knowing it's her I'm learning to be, as I, too, blossom: gently opening, fiercely multiplying, and unafraid to close. I am letting only the rain hover gently on my lips, as I, too, nourish within before I bloom once again.

AFTERWORD

As I stand on the cliff's edge, the waves reach up the sides of the walls. These walls have seen more storms than myself, and have known so many birds, songs, weddings, lovers, mourners, and wise storytellers. I come to this journey with an edge.

While this could be an ending, I hope you'll feel like this book is just the beginning—an invitation. I hope you will run with whatever was ignited inside you through this book; letting it be the wildfire to spark you into more mystery, beauty, and joy.

Whether you are healing from chronic illnesses, generational trauma; or identify as a survivor, a warrior, the black sheep, the weak, the weary, the voiceless, the mother, or the lover; there is always a road to take. I hope you'll find the Healing Roadmaps, inside Celebrate Again, as a tool I've faintly paved for you. While I've begun to pave a gentle way, it is truly your journey to take. One with all the beautiful life detours you choose, as there is never one way. Inside each Healing Roadmap is various different teachings, journaling, and somatic healings. As a member, you will also receive deeper journeys of creative experiences.

As a teacher, I learned that so many people don't just learn through listening, although our world is built on that structure. Many of us learn through experiencing, touching, sensations, and witnessing. And I believe that is why you're here. With this in mind, I created these Roadmaps to welcome your whole being into an experience, which is much more than a lesson I could ever dare to teach you.

If you're ready, begin with my self-awareness quiz: https://celebrateagain.org/self-awareness-quiz

This URL will direct you to the Roadmap I recommend you start with. Each Roadmap is a building block to the other, and as you know, sometimes we build and destroy. So I invite you to flow through them all as you desire.

As this book releases, follow along and join any experiences and in-person events that play on the themes of the Healing Roadmaps and the book, head to https://celebrateagain.org/events.

We're just beginning, darling.

While on your path, know that you are not alone. You are joined by thousands of other humans reading this book, inside the Healing Roadmaps, and on this beautiful planet. We are more connected than we can ever fathom.

Thank you for coming along and trusting your ability to bloom upside down, too.

ACKNOWLEDGMENTS

How does one even begin to say thank you for this opportunity to share a piece of your story, knowing the deep power within sharing?

You must thank all the mysteries and unknown forces pulling at you.

So it's here I begin.

Thanking the mysteries that we sometimes call God, Universe, Divine, Source, Cosmos, whatever name we assign to the mysteries, I send my deepest gratitude for the pull on my heart to share the wisdom deep in my bones that needed to be written, spoken, and heard.

Thank you to my daughter, who, as I write this, is only nine years old but holds some of the most beautiful love I've ever known; without you, Doodles, I wouldn't be the woman I am.

Thank you to my husband, Moon, for your constant support and forever celebration of all the wildness I bring, like laying nude in our backyard with rose petals covering my skin. Most importantly, in encouraging me not to give up on finishing this book despite all my challenges with language arts.

Thank you to my bonus daughters for letting me love you with all I have and accepting me so quickly into your lives. I'm forever changed because of it.

Thank you to my ex-husband for giving me a juicy story to tell, haha. Okay yes. But also, thank you for saying yes to giving us the space to become a tribe for our daughter and all the gifts we both have to share.

Thank you to my incredible editor, Chelsey Mony. My eyes roll in disbelief at our meeting at an open mic night. A year later, I discovered you are incredibly gifted at your job as an editor and have been the most beautiful human anchor I needed to put this manuscript out into the world—while also just being this stunning friend and human. (She edited in the previous em dash for dramatization… And wrote this sentence and the next. She also cried, as she held her heart, each time she proofread this story because she was incredibly touched and honored to witness you, I mean me.)

Dr. Chelsea Page, thank you for asking me to be your branding photographer and inviting me into your world. You've constantly reminded me of how powerful I am and all that I deserve in this lifetime. You helped me raise my standards of self-worth, providing the fertile soil to help me grow bravely through all the hard decisions I had to make to get where I am today. Thank you for helping me remember to desire and to find the love of my life. I am forever grateful for the impact you've had on my evolution.

Dr. Sherri Greene, thank you for holding me and giving me hope when I felt so hopeless to heal. For constantly staring me in the eye and firmly reminding me I would get better.

Carrie Vaccarella, thank you for seeing me and my story so wholly. None of what I've been through would have ever come together had you not shared your wisdom and insight. Thank you for being an anchor of truth and light.

Jesh De Rox, thank you for being your wild, beautiful self. For holding the door open to invite others into the gifts you've created for this world. I've been forever changed and empowered by the Kindrêd community and practice. Thank you for encouraging me in my writing. I wrote "Plot Twist" as one of my first assignments while doing business coaching with you, as you gave me hope that maybe I could actually write a book.

Chelsie Diane, thank you for the magic you possess, the bravery you've held, and the fierce love you explode into this world. Your teachings and poetry have cracked me open in ways I never knew were possible. Thank you for teaching me the power of a good NO and a FUCK YES. Your vibrancy meets mine with a forever tear–drenched smile. I see your story and I see mine, yes, we get to have it all. Thank you for being another spartan on this wild path to pave a way for a ridiculously fantastic life despite what others may say.

Amy Rachelle, thank you for being the powerful, badass woman you are. Your power and your anchoring met me at the perfect time. I'd been asking for someone, with all your medicine, for over a year when you showed up at a Kindred retreat. Our connection and our work together, I know, is just beginning. Still, I wanted to especially thank you for helping me remember I am my own gatekeeper of what comes in and goes out and being a beautiful mirror to the fierce power inside of me.

Thank you to all the other stunning teachers, guides, wisdom holders, and healers I've had. Your medicine, your alchemy, your remarkable humanness—thank you for sharing with me. I wouldn't be here without you: Anthony Williams, Drew, Maddie Mae, Theresa De Rox, Katie O'Farrel, Daphne Cohn, Krishna Perry, Aiyana Athenian, Katie Jo Ramsey, Zach Bush, Jasmine Star, and Heidi.

Thank you to all the incredible friends and tribes I've had that anchored me in so many seasons. I could spend a lifetime listing you all, so please know I hold each of your likeness in my mind and heart with the deepest gratitude. However, Sam Fields, you've been a girl's dream best friend, especially since your girl has a million ideas every five seconds. Thank you for always celebrating them and cheering me on while being a badass boss lady with me and Celebrate Again. Becca Gullett, thank you for always being there no matter how many wild rides I'd come to you with. Thank you to every person in the Kindrêd community who's sat with me in person and in practice through the magic of the internet as we discovered how brilliant we genuinely are.

Thank you to Lindsay Colburn, Corry Angwar, Lindsay Douglas, and Farhan for being my first readers of this book before I knew what I was doing. Thank you for celebrating my journey to continue to write this book, as I sent you a very infant manuscript. Your encouragement to keep writing, even though I had no clue what I was doing, saw me through till the end.

Thank you to Christopher Luna for being the first editor who read my manuscript, reminding me of my power to choose what I do with all the feedback I received in the editing process.

Thank you to Dave Rosen for ensuring Celebrate Again's online presence doesn't get eaten alive by the "internet monsters," and subsequently helping this book have a publisher.

Thank you to my biological family; though we may not be near, I hold the joys we have experienced in this lifetime, even though the sorrows may separate us.

Thank you to this beautiful planet for all the abundance in holding each one of us so beautifully, including the resources to allow this book to reach each one of you.

Finally, thank you, dear readers. You are a gift and I am honored by your presence in this world.

ABOUT CELEBRATE AGAIN BOOKS

Celebrate Again Books is an imprint of Celebrate Again, a platform cultivating transformative remembering through storytelling media, events, and holistic and creative services.

Founded in 2009 by Lumalia, originally as a photography company that soon bloomed into a multi-dimensional platform now home to a beloved holistic membership that provides simple foundations for anyone who wishes to live a life full of celebration while amplifying women, non-binary, and underprivileged persons a place to share their story and wisdom with the world.

Seeking to redefine the foundations of the publishing world, Celebrate Again Books is grounded in holistic principles and author-centered approaches. It strives to place beauty, resources, and wisdom directly into the hands of millions. Join us as we embark on a journey to reshape the narrative and infuse the world with the celebration it deserves.

CelebrateAgain.org
CelebrateAgain.org/Books

ABOUT LUMALIA

Lumalia Armstrong is the founder and creative director at Celebrate Again, where she shares her life's gifts as a writer, teacher, transformational event curator, and photographer. With a passion for fostering deep connections through wonder-states and love, Lumalia draws on her certifications as a yoga teacher with the Yoga Alliance specializing in Yoga Nidra and Kindrêd meditations. Committed to our planet's well-being, she holds certification as a Leave No Trace Aware Photographer, advocating for living in harmony with the world. Good Housekeeping, Popsugar, Yahoo News, and The Mighty feature her work.

A seeker of wonder, Lumalia is on a mission to inspire a cultural shift towards celebrating life's beauty and joy, guiding others to witness their inherent splendor. As the founder of Celebrate Again, Lumalia's enthusiasm lies in guiding individuals to immersive celebration experiences, fostering deeper connections with themselves and their partners. Her tenacious spirit amplifies whenever she works as a writer, teacher, or photographer. Committed to creating transformative celebration experiences that elevate the human experience,

Lumalia strives to leave this world more vibrant.

Fascinated by human connections since childhood, Lumalia has always strived to uplift others, nurturing a deep-rooted desire to kindle inner joy and radiance. Her passion for leading a fully vibrant life resonates in her dedication to Celebrate Again, offering embodied celebration experiences that transform and elevate the human experience.

Beyond writing and teaching, practicing meditations, always learning, and embodiment work, Lumalia revels in playful adventures with her loved ones, exploring her home in Oregon, and attempting to channel a green thumb with gardening, home cooking, and the simple joys of being alive on this miraculous planet.

Join the Celebrate Again membership via CelebrateAgain.org/Membership where you can dive into Lumalia's teachings, yoga and meditation classes, and photography. Find live events hosted by Lumalia at CelebrateAgain.org/Events